Everyman, I will go with thee,
and be thy guide

THE EVERYMAN
LIBRARY

The Everyman Library was founded by J. M. Dent
in 1906. He chose the name Everyman because he wanted
to make available the best books ever written in every
field to the greatest number of people at the cheapest possible
price. He began with Boswell's 'Life of Johnson';
his one-thousandth title was Aristotle's 'Metaphysics',
by which time sales exceeded forty million.

Today Everyman paperbacks remain true to
J. M. Dent's aims and high standards, with a wide range
of titles at affordable prices in editions which address
the needs of today's readers. Each new text is reset to give
a clear, elegant page and to incorporate the latest thinking
and scholarship. Each book carries the pilgrim logo,
the character in 'Everyman', a medieval mystery play,
a proud link between Everyman
past and present.

Niccolò Machiavelli

THE PRINCE
AND OTHER POLITICAL
WRITINGS

Translated and edited by
STEPHEN J. MILNER
University of Bristol

Consultant Editor for this volume
ROBIN KIRKPATRICK
Robinson College, Cambridge

EVERYMAN
J. M. DENT · LONDON
CHARLES E. TUTTLE
VERMONT

Introduction, notes and other critical apparatus
© J M Dent 1995

First published in Everyman in 1908

This edition first published in 1995
All rights reserved

J. M. Dent
Orion Publishing Group
Orion House, 5 Upper St Martin's Lane,
London WC2H 9EA
and
Charles E. Tuttle Co., Inc.
28 South Main Street,
Rutland, Vermont 05701, USA

Typeset in Sabon by CentraCet Ltd
Printed in Great Britain by
The Guernsey Press Co. Ltd, Guernsey, C. I.

British Library Cataloguing-in-Publication Data
is available upon request.

ISBN 0 460 87629 5

CONTENTS

To Nicola,
with love

NOTE ON THE AUTHOR AND
TRANSLATOR AND EDITOR

NICCOLÒ DI BERNARDO MACHIAVELLI, Florentine, civil servant, political analyst and playwright, lived through a watershed in Italian history. His lifetime stretched from the accession to power of Lorenzo *il Magnifico* de' Medici in Florence (1469) to the Sack of Rome (1527). During that time he saw four changes of government within Florence, the invasion of Italy by the French and then by the Imperial forces. He was implicated in two political conspiracies, imprisoned, tortured, exiled and partially reintegrated into political life. During the height of his diplomatic career in the Second Chancery, and under the patronage of Piero Soderini, he was sent on missions to the King of France, the Holy Roman Emperor in Germany, the Pope in Rome, as well as a host of other potentates within Italy itself. He witnessed the burning of Savonarola and the rise and fall of Cesare Borgia. In his own lifetime he was more renowned as a comic playwright. He was a copious and entertaining correspondent whose more formal writings were the result of periods of enforced leisure imposed upon him by changing political fortunes. Always keen to be involved in events, his observations on politics, religion and human nature were based on a potent mix of personal experience and a reading of the ancients. A writer on principalities and republics, a poet and letter-writer, an historian and comic playwright, Machiavelli was provocative, proud and direct. His writings are a vivid interpretation of the culture of his times.

STEPHEN J. MILNER is Lecturer in Italian Studies at the University of Bristol, and has written articles and reviews on Machiavelli, Renaissance political rhetoric, the patronage of Lorenzo de' Medici and the Florentine territorial state.

CHRONOLOGY OF THE
LIFE AND TIMES OF MACHIAVELLI

1469	3 May	Niccolò born to Bernardo Machiavelli and Bartolomea de' Nelli. His father was a lawyer of little note and not eligible for political office under Florentine rules governing political eligibility.
	December	Piero de' Medici dies, and is succeeded as head of the Medici family by his son Lorenzo *Il Magnifico*.
1478		Pazzi conspiracy. Giuliano de' Medici, brother of Lorenzo, murdered in Florence.
1490		Fra Girolamo Savonarola, the Dominican friar, returns to Florence, his evangelical preaching attracting a considerable following.
1492	8 April	Lorenzo de Medici dies, and is succeeded by his son Piero (1471–1503). Alessandro VI, a Borgia, elected Pope.
1494	September	Charles VIII, King of France, invades Italy to pursue his claims on the Kingdom of Naples. Piero de' Medici exiled by the Florentines, who declare a new Republic. Savonarola's influence extends to the political life of the city.
1498	18 February	Machiavelli is nominated as a candidate for the post of Secretary to the Second Chancery. He is defeated by followers of Savonarola.
	9 March	Machiavelli writes letter to Ricciardo Becchi, Florentine Ambassador in Rome, criticising Savonarola.
	23 May	Savonarola tried, hanged and burnt in the Piazza della Signoria in Florence for heresy.
	19 June	Machiavelli is elected to post of Secretary to the Second Chancery, the department responsible for the administration of the Florentine territorial state. In addition, on 14 July he also took up a post as Secretary to the Ten of War, the body responsible for Florentine foreign affairs.

1499	March–July	Machiavelli completes his first diplomatic missions to Jacopo d'Appiano, signore of Piombino, and Caterina Sforza, Countess of Forlí. Writes the brief *Report on the Pisan War*
1500	July	Machiavelli is sent on a mission to France on behalf of the Florentines to express to Louis XII Florentine resentment at the mutiny of the French troops responsible for the siege of Pisa.
1501		Further missions to Pistoia, Cascina and Siena. In the autumn he married Marietta di Luigi Corsini; they had four sons and a daughter.
1502	June	Cesare Borgia, the Duke Valentino, seizes the duchy of Urbino from Guidobaldo da Montefeltro, the Duke of Urbino. Machiavelli accompanies Francesco Soderini on a mission to Urbino. Machiavelli's first encounter with Cesare Borgia.
	26 August	Piero Soderini elected 'Gonfaloniere of Florence' for life, in the hope that it would provide increased internal stability in Florence.
	October	Machiavelli sent to Borgia again after the rebellion of Vitellozzo Vitelli, the Orsini and others against the Duke. The rebels all gathered at Magione to monitor developments
1503	January	Borgia dramatically murders the conspirators, and Machiavelli sends a report back to the *Signori* in Florence which was to provide the basis for his subsequent tract, *Duke Valentino's Treacherous Betrayal of Vitellozzo Vitelli, Oliverotto da Fermo and Others*.
	March–June	Writes *Remarks on the Raising of Money* and *How to Deal with the People of the Valdichiana who have Rebelled*, both on the subject of seeking to pacify the uprisings within the Florentine territories.
	18 August	Pope Alexander VI dies, his successor, Pope Pius III, also dying in October of the same year. Machiavelli sent to Rome to observe the conclave. Giuliano della Rovere is elected Pope Julius II, and promptly withdraws support for Cesare Borgia whose fortunes decline.
1504	January	Machiavelli sent to France with Niccolò Valori to negotiate terms of alliance with Louis XII. Wrote *The First Decade*, a verse account of events in Italy between 1494–1504.

1505	September	Florence is defeated in the siege of Pisa. Machiavelli, with Soderini's support, begins to work on plans for the institution of a Florentine civic militia.
1506	December	Machiavelli becomes Secretary of the newly created Nine of Militia responsible for the organising of citizen militia. Writes his *Discourse on Florentine Military Preparation*.
1507	December	Machiavelli is sent by Soderini to join Francesco Vettori on a mission to the Emperor Maximilian in Germany. Their purpose was to gain assurances that the Florentine territorial state would remain untouched in the Emperor's attempts to regain the lands taken by the Venetians.
1508	June	Returns to Florence and writes *A Report on German Affairs*, reworked in 1509 as *Discourse on German Affairs and the Emperor*, and finally in 1512 as *A Portrait of German Affairs*.
	10 December	League of Cambrai is signed by a coalition of states against the Venetians.
1509		Machiavelli is involved in the organisation of the continuing conflict with Pisa.
1510	February	Pope Julius II, in a volte-face, concludes an alliance with the Venetians leading to tension between France and the Pope.
	June	Machiavelli sent to France to mediate between the Pope and Louis XII.
	October	Machiavelli returns to Florence. Writes *A Portrait of French Affairs* around this time.
	23 December	Discovery in Florence of the Prinzivalle della Stufa plot against Soderini.
1511		Louis XII decides to call a convocation of francophile cardinals to depose the Pope.
	August	Pope Julius II reported gravely ill. Soderini decides to back the pro-French cardinals. The Pope makes an unexpected recovery.
	September	Machiavelli sent to Milan and France to petition Louis XII to suspend the convocation of the schismatic francophile cardinals at the Council of Pisa. Julius II issues an interdict against Florence.
	4 October	The Pope forms the Holy League against the French, with Venice, the Empire and Spain, and favours Medici exiles.

1512	11 April	The French win the battle of Ravenna, but fail to consolidate the victory and are eventually forced to withdraw their forces from Milan, leaving Florence exposed and without allies.
	29 August	The Holy League's army takes Prato from the militia.
	1 September	Soderini is deposed and Giuliano de' Medici enters Florence.
	7 November	Machiavelli is removed from office in favour of Niccolò Michelozzi, a Medicean, and is exiled to the Florentine territory shortly afterwards for one year with a surety of one thousand gold florins.
1513	February	Machiavelli is implicated in a plot to overthrow the Medici. He is arrested, tortured and held in prison. He is released as part of a general amnesty consequent upon Giovanni de' Medici being elected Pope Leo X.
	April	Machiavelli begins a correspondence with Francesco Vettori in Rome.
	10 December	Machiavelli mentions to Vettori the near completion of a short tract entitled *De principatibus (On Principalities)*.
1514–?		Machiavelli writes his *Discourse or Dialogue on our Language* on or around this time.
1516	March	Giuliano de' Medici's death leaves his nephew Lorenzo di Piero de' Medici (1492–1519) in charge of Florence, and Machiavelli's *Il principe* without a dedicatee. Machiavelli dedicates it to the young Lorenzo who had occupied Urbino as Captain-General of the Papal and Florentine forces that same month.
1516–17		Machiavelli frequents the *Orti Oricellari* group in Florence and completes his commentary on Livy, the *Discourses on the First Ten Books of Titus Livy*.
1518		Machiavelli writes the black comedy *The Mandragola*. Also of this period are the prose story *Belfagor* and *The Golden Ass*.
1519	4 May	The young Lorenzo de' Medici dies. Machiavelli starts work on *The Art of War*, which he completes the following year.

1520		Machiavelli writes *The Discourse on Florentine Affairs after the Death of Lorenzo de' Medici the Younger*, at the invitation of Cardinal Giulio de' Medici. Machiavelli is also sent to Lucca on a private mission on behalf of a group of Florentine merchants. He writes *A Summary of the Affairs of the City of Lucca* and the *Life of Castruccio Castracani*.
	8 November	Machiavelli receives the commission to write *The Florentine Histories*.
1523		Cardinal Giulio de' Medici is elected Pope as Clement VII after the death of Leo X and Adrian VI.
1525		Machiavelli writes his second comedy, *La Clizia*, and finishes *The Florentine Histories*, which he presents to Clement VII in May.
1526		The League of Cognac comprising the Papacy, France, Venice and Milan is formed against Charles V. Machiavelli is partly responsible for ensuring the fortification of Florence and is nominated one of Five Procurators of the Walls.
1527	May	The sack of Rome by Imperial forces. The Florentines revolt against the Medici and establish a new republic. Machiavelli rushes back to Florence, but is excluded from holding any office on account of his perceived collaboration with Medici patrons.
	21 June	Machiavelli dies in poverty surrounded by a few friends.

INTRODUCTION

The historical context

The final chapter of Machiavelli's *The Prince* is entitled 'An Exhortation to Seize Italy and Free her from the Barbarians'. In the preceding chapters, Machiavelli examines the causes of Italy's weakness and suggests remedies. As he states in the dedicatory letter to the young Lorenzo de' Medici these remedies were derived from a mixture of his own experiences as a diplomat in the service of the Florentine republic and a prudent reading of the ancient writers. In 1513, at the time of writing, Italy had been subject to several recent foreign incursions. In 1494 Charles VIII of France had descended into Italy in order to pursue a claim to the Kingdom of Naples which he successfully took in 1495. In subsequent Italian histories, this precedent became seen as the symbolic moment of Italy's final ruination which led inexorably to the Sack of Rome by the forces of Charles V, King of Spain and Holy Roman Emperor, in May 1527. In the intervening years Italy was invaded by King Louis XII of France who joined with the Venetians to occupy Milan and expel Ludovico Sforza in 1499; by King Ferdinand of Aragon who joined with Louis XII to seize Naples from Ferdinand's cousin Frederick I; and by the Holy Roman Emperor Maximilian between 1507–15. The formation of the Holy League against the French in 1511 saw an alliance of the Papacy with the Venetians, the Empire and Spain, only Florence remaining steadfast in its support of the French. For the patriotic Machiavelli such barbarian interference in Italian affairs was hard to countenance. As it was, Italy had to await the *Risorgimento* of the nineteenth century before finally ridding herself of foreign occupiers.

These interventions upset the precarious political balance that had existed within Italy until that time. Historically fragmented, Italy was politically divided with no overall power exercising exclusive domination. In the south was the Kingdom of Naples, in the centre the Papal States that spread from Rome as far as Bologna, and in the north the duchy of Milan, whilst Venice and Florence were the two most powerful republics. In addition there was a host of smaller states from the duchy of Urbino to the republics of Lucca and Siena. The Papal States, however, were by no means under the political control of the Papacy, with particular families exercising princely authority over major towns like Bologna and Perugia, ruled by the Bentivogli and Baglioni respectively. Apart from the foreign armies, the major military player in Italy from 1494 to 1513 was the Papacy, initially under the dynamic leadership Pope Alexander VI and his son Cesare Borgia and then under Julius II. Borgia's campaigns during the period 1499 to 1503 re-established papal control over the Romagna and the Marche, and added to the instability within the peninsula, with Florence especially fearful of Borgia's territorial ambitions and his sympathy with the Medici exiles. It was in this context that Machiavelli came into contact with Borgia, the Duke Valentino, who became a central character in *The Prince* and the subject of Machiavelli's admiration.

These changes in the political balance of power within Italy itself had a major impact on Machiavelli's native city, Florence. Machiavelli was born in May 1469, the year Lorenzo (*il Magnifico*) de' Medici (1449–92) assumed pre-eminence in Florence after his father's death. Although Florence was nominally still a republic, the Medici family had established political hegemony by setting up an extensive patronage network and controlling the elections to the major offices of state. However, with the descent of Charles VIII into Italy in 1494, the Florentines expelled Lorenzo's heir, Piero de' Medici (1471–1503), and instituted a new republic, more broadly based and under the evangelical guidance of the Dominican friar Girolamo Savonarola. Florence became split by internal divisions within the ruling élite, and Savonarola's influence waned when he was excommunicated for his constant criticism of Catholic corruption. Hanged and burned in the Piazza della Signoria in May 1498, Savonarola's death added to the internal tensions. In September 1502 it was finally decided, in the hope of providing stability, to modify the leading political post within the republic, that of the *gonfaloniere di giustizia*, making it an appointment for life in imitation of the Doge in Venice. Piero Soderini was elected and held the post until the return of the Medici to Florence in 1512, when the exiled Giuliano (1479–1516) and Giovanni de' Medici (1475–1521) returned to the city.

Machiavelli's own life was profoundly affected by these events, indeed they had a crucial bearing on his own political fortune. His election to his first executive post was a result of the purge of Savonarolan supporters from public offices in 1498, and under the patronage of Piero Soderini he reached a position of diplomatic importance previously unimaginable for a man of his social rank. With the return of the Medici in 1512, however, he found himself dismissed from office due to his association with the previous regime.

At the time of writing *The Prince*, therefore, Machiavelli was in exile from Florence, excluded from holding any kind of office, and conscious of the steadily increasing power of the Medici not only in Florence but also in Rome. In February 1513 Cardinal Giovanni de' Medici, second son of Lorenzo *il Magnifico*, was elected Pope Leo X. Machiavelli's correspondence with his former diplomatic colleague under Soderini, Francesco Vettori (then ambassador to the Papal court in Rome), clearly indicates his impatience to re-enter the political fray. Removed from active participation, Machiavelli had time to dwell on, and write about, the dramatic events of the previous twenty years. *The Prince* is the result of that contemplation, and the product of an epistolary dialogue with Vettori concerning Italy's political ills. His aim was to regain employment of some kind, and it seemed fitting that Giuliano de' Medici, who had just re-entered Florence, should be the dedicatee of this small work filled with advice for a new prince recently come to power. Machiavelli's hope was that this new prince could provide unity and strength in Italy, and so prevent a repetition of the tragic events of the previous twenty years, and further 'barbarian' invasions.

Life and works

Machiavelli was born into a family that was not part of the political élite. His father Bernardo was a struggling lawyer and Machiavelli one of four children. Yet he received a standard humanist education, starting with elementary Latin at the age of seven and proceeding to more advanced study of Latin authors with the aid of a series of private tutors. In all probability he attended lectures at the Florentine *studio*, the city's university. His father's diary refers to a small family library of classical works, including Livy, and Machiavelli has been identified as the copyist of a manuscript of Lucretius dated in the 1490s. Little more is known of his youth until he was elected second chancellor, on 19 June 1498. The Chancery was the department responsible for the administration of the republic's internal and external affairs, carrying out the decisions reached by the politically franchised citizens in the city's councils and magistracies. The second chancellor was nominally responsible for the administration of affairs within the Florentine territorial state, which at that time covered large areas of Tuscany and parts of Umbria, from Livorno to Volterra and Cortona. In July of the same year Machiavelli was granted the additional job within the chancery of serving the *Dieci di Balìa*, or Ten of War, and later in 1507 he was made chancellor of the Nine of the Militia. These posts were all permanent administrative positions, unlike the political posts which rotated at regular intervals in line with the republican constitution.

Machiavelli's active service in the Florentine chancery lasted for over fourteen years, and involved him in meeting many of the leading political figures of the day. Although his role was nominally executive, he did more than prepare letters and write minutes. He often accompanied ambassadors on diplomatic missions in service of the republic, going to France in 1500,

1504 and 1510–11, and Germany in 1507. Within Italy itself he was constantly away from Florence on governmental business, both in the territorial state and beyond. In 1502–3 he spent a significant and formative period in the company of Cesare Borgia. The experiences gathered during that period provided the basis for his early political writings, and the observations and the maxims they contain find their way, in modified form, into the argument of *The Prince* itself. His reflections on Cesare Borgia in the piece on the rebellion of the Valdichiana suggest an early appreciation of Borgia's daring, whilst his writings on Germany and France illustrate his interest in the variety of political forms, and their respective military and institutional strengths and weaknesses.

Machiavelli was most productive during his enforced leisure after the return of the Medici to Florence. He first mentions *The Prince* to Vettori in late 1513, but there is no certainty that the volume even found its way to its eventual dedicatee, Lorenzo de' Medici the younger (1492–1519). One story relates that the young prince was more interested in a pair of greyhounds presented to him at the same time. Machiavelli became increasingly impatient with his own failure to win the trust and patronage of the Medici family, and it was not until 1526, a year prior to his death that he was made one of the five officials appointed to oversee the fortification of Florence. His writing continued unabated, however, and he frequented the *Orti Oricellari* group of liberal patricians which met, as the name suggests, in the gardens of Cosimo Rucellai. They encouraged Machiavelli's literary endeavours, providing some financial support, and as a consequence he dedicated his republican commentary, the *Discourses on the First Ten Books of Titus Livy*, to two of their number: Cosimo Rucellai and Zanobi Buondelmonti.

In 1518 and 1519 Machiavelli wrote *The Art of War* and his black comedy, *La Mandragola*. Finally, in 1520 the Medici's attitude seemed to soften, with Cardinal Giulio de' Medici asking him to write a tract on the best form of government for Florence, the result being the *Discourse on Florentine Affairs after the Death of Lorenzo de Medici the Younger.* Later that year Giulio also commissioned him to write *The Florentine Histories*, a commission he completed in 1525. During the same period he wrote another play, *La Clizia*, and a couple of tracts based on his visit to Lucca in 1520.

The final ironic twist in Machiavelli's career, however, happened in 1527 – the last year of his life. Once again the Medici had been driven from Florence in the wake of the invading Imperial forces, and once again Florence embraced a republican government. Machiavelli was proposed as a candidate to fill the vacant office of the secretary to the Ten, a position he had formerly held under the previous republic. Yet despite the support of friends from the *Oricellari* group he was not elected, and he died shortly afterwards at the age of fifty-eight, rejected by the new republicans, his own life a case study in the vagaries of political fortune.

The literary context

Machiavelli's *The Prince* stands in a long tradition of 'Mirror of Princes' handbooks. During the Renaissance this type of manual was commonly written and presented to rulers by humanists. Such texts were a mixture of classical and religious elements which, by the time of Petrarch (1304–74), combined Christian morality with classical examples. Addressed to the person of the prince, they were exhortations to virtuous government on the part of the prince, set within the rhetorical tradition of praise and blame, outlining the virtues to be followed and vices to be avoided if a prince were to become glorious.

In seeking to clarify Machiavelli's relation to, and critique of, this tradition, it is worth providing an outline of its conventions through an examination of a typical example of its genre: Petrarch's letter to Francesco Carrara, ruler of Padua, of 1373.[1]

---

[1] Quotations are taken from the English translation by B. G. Kohl in *The Earthly Republic: Italian Humanists on Government and Society*, ed., B. G. Kohl and R. G. Witt (Manchester, 1978), pp. 33–78.

Entitled *How a Ruler Ought to Govern His State*, Petrarch's letter defines the function of such texts in clarifying the duties of the ruler to his subjects, and cites Cicero, Suetonius and biblical references to add authority to his message. The text, as suggested by the genre's title, was to act as a kind of mirror, a source of self-reflection for the prince, '. . . I want you to look at yourself in this letter as though you were gazing in a mirror' (p. 41). Should the prince notice any differences between himself and the image of a virtuous ruler found within the pages of the text, Petrarch says, 'I advise you to put your hands to your face and polish the countenance of your great reputation written there, so that you might become more attractive, and certainly more illustrious, as a result of this experience' (pp. 41–2).

These texts, therefore, sought to educate a prince in good government and help him win fame and glory. Glory inevitably followed in the wake of virtue, so it was important the prince understood the benefits and dangers of the respective virtues and vices; for example justice, generosity and compassion, and their opposites, cruelty, avarice and ingratitude. Citing Cicero's *On Duties*, Petrarch notes that the love of the people is the prince's best and surest defence, whilst also warning of the dangers of acting in a way that will render him contemptible in their eyes. The prince was to love his people, and assume the role of *pater patriae* (father of the country), the classical tag bestowed on emperors of antiquity and later on Cosimo de' Medici in Florence. This was one of many similar paternalistic governmental analogies that involved the ruler sublimating his own interests for the good of his subjects. Others described the ideal prince as like a captain of a ship, a shepherd or a teacher. Metaphors of the body politic also abounded, the prince representing the head of state, or in the case of Petrarch, the heart.

The way the prince was perceived by the people is vital in these exhortations to virtuous living. Citing examples from Cicero, Claudian and Livy, Petrarch says: 'Every people strives to imitate the deeds and habits of its prince. Hence, there is that very true saying that there is nothing more harmful to the state than the bad example of its prince' (pp. 72–3). The causal relationship, therefore, was clear and linear. The prince's subjects were his audience, their behaviour affected by his. Consequently, he had a moral obligation to embody the virtues considered indispensable to a ruler. Once the prince had read the book, reflected on its contents, and noticed any disparities between himself and the perfect self described, he should seek to alter his metaphorical garments and features in order to accord with the image presented, thereby becoming a living example of virtue that his people could imitate. This was the road to glory.

Petrarch's is only one example of the genre, but it is fairly typical in its format and conclusions. Others were written and presented to princes by fifteenth-century humanists such as Patrizi, Bracciolini, Sacchi, Carafa and Pontano. *The Prince* should be read as a critique of this tradition of humanist writing on princely government. The irony is that *The Prince* is the most famous and yet the least typical of the genre. Most of these tracts were presented to hereditary rulers, who were members of well-established ruling dynasties. Machiavelli's was addressed to a new prince. In the turbulent world of Italian politics in the early sixteenth century it was possible for people to become rulers who had little or no experience of government and had not been trained in its methods.

The argument

Machiavelli was one of a number of writers, including Vettori's brother Paulo, who encouraged the Medici to adopt a princely form of government on their return to Florence in 1512. Machiavelli first made mention of the text in his letter to Vettori of 10 December 1513, referring to it in Latin as *De principatibus* (*On Principalities*). This in itself points to one of the salient features of the piece that differentiates it from the 'Mirror of Princes' genre. Rather than solely addressing the person of the prince, Machiavelli first concentrated on the different types of state a prince could acquire, as this was what conditioned his subsequent behaviour. It is not until Chapter 15 that Machiavelli engaged fully with the traditional issue of the virtues and vices a prince should follow and avoid. For Machiavelli, the overarching concern of a new ruler was to '*mantenere lo stato*' (maintain his rule), protecting himself from internal and external threat. A newly acquired state was the most difficult to secure in this respect, as there was initially a greater possibility of being ousted. The aim of a new prince, therefore, was to secure his rule as quickly as possible, and appear well founded and of long standing. To do this, Machiavelli explained, he, as author, had to go behind (*andare dietro*) the imagined states described by former writers to examine the reality of the matter, as the new prince had to deal with how men behaved in practice rather than concern himself with how they should behave in theory.

The success of the prince in achieving permanency of rule depended in large part on his own personal ability, what Machiavelli refers to as his *virtù*. The term is derived from the Latin *vir* meaning man and allied to *vis* meaning strength. Although it can be used to denote virtue in both the Christian sense (faith, hope and charity) and the classical sense (justice, prudence, temperance and fortitude), the term is used more broadly by Machiavelli to denote a personal ability which is dynamic, strong, daring and manly. The extent of the *virtù* required by a new prince depends on the amount of work required to secure himself in his new possession. Using an artistic analogy, Machiavelli states that the prince must form the *materia*, or the matter, of state to ensure his security. When at all possible, a new prince should leave as much as possible of the previous form intact, its language, customs and institutions. The less disturbance caused in entering a state, the less potential exists for others to seek further change. This is why Machiavelli ignores hereditary principalities, as they are already formed, a change of ruler merely involving the substitution of one prince for another within a pre-existent structure. In other cases, however, a prince may need to destroy the previous form totally in order to secure himself, a task that requires a proportional increase in his *virtù*. Consequently constructional metaphors abound in the text, all relating to the active, forming quality of *virtù*.

This quality of *virtù*, however, is not only the quality that enables a prince to secure himself, but is also what enables him to acquire the *materia* of state in the first instance. *Virtù* is closely allied to the related key concepts of *occasione* (opportunity) and *fortuna*. A *virtuoso* prince, therefore, is one who seizes the opportunity presented by fortune to acquire another's state. He must then use his *virtù* to secure himself against those who are likewise seeking an opportunity to innovate (*innovare*), namely, to bring about political change. In Chapter 24 Machiavelli observes that double glory is due to a prince who manages to do this, not only acquiring a principality, but also successfully forming and securing it.

Machiavelli rejects the kind of stoical resignation to the fates expressed by Vettori in his letter of 23 November 1513, preferring to see man's ability to shape his own ends as a constant struggle between the dynamic, active and constructive qualities of *virtù* and the fickle, destructive and female quality of *fortuna*. Fortune represents the ever-changing political environment which the prince inhabits. He must act or risk being acted upon. As a woman, Fortune, says Machiavelli, prefers courageous young men who are bold and treat her roughly. In the words of the proverb, 'fortune favours the brave.' A prince must therefore seek to control fortune, prevent her from deserting him. This requires that he be able to alter his policies as circumstances dictate, constantly reacting to the changes around him. An inability to alter his behaviour will inevitably lead to his ruin. Not surprisingly the text is full of metaphors of restraint and control: bridling, chaining, holding firm, governing – all terms that refer to the controlling of circumstance and the vagaries of fortune.

To limit fortune's power and thereby increase his own security, a prince should depend on nobody but himself and his own *virtù*. Any obligation, any debt, any power shared with another is a source of weakness and potential ruin. As he states at the end of Chapter 24, 'the only defences that are good, that are certain, and that are durable are those that depend solely on oneself and on one's own strength and ability [*virtù*]'. Italy's mistake was to rely on mercenaries and the military forces that belonged to others. Machiavelli sees everyone, princes, nobles and the people, as self-interested and fickle, constantly in search of an improvement in their material circumstances. Machiavelli, like Petrarch, believed the love of the people was a prince's surest defence, but that love alone was insufficient, as people are self-interested. The prince must be able to secure them more firmly in their allegiance to him. It is easy to persuade people to be loyal and identify their interests with his, but difficult to maintain them in that persuasion. Consequently the prince needs access to force. In a wry allusion to Savonarola, Machiavelli observes that unarmed prophets perish.

Machiavelli's prince is not the personification of evil that his reputation would have us believe. As far as is possible a prince should be virtuous, should have the qualities outlined in the moral tracts mentioned above, but when necessity dictates otherwise, he should be able to act in a non-virtuous manner to preserve himself. Necessity will periodically constrain the prince to act like this to survive. It is part of the prince's *virtù* to recognise when those moments arise and know how to act accordingly. Machiavelli observes that what is presented as a virtue in the pedagogical tracts of other writers, when placed within the framework of the need to stay in power could lead to a prince's ruin. A prince, 'will find that something which seems virtue can, if put into practice, cause his ruin, while another thing that seems a vice, can when put into practice, result in his security and well-being'. What Machiavelli does here is make a political virtue of necessity.

The prince, therefore, needs to develop the dual traits of the fox and the lion, employing guile and force to secure himself. The strength of the lion will deter external powers and defend him from internal threat. The guile and craftiness of the fox will enable him to avoid traps and dissimulate. For if the prince is to gain a good reputation he must be seen to be virtuous even if, at times, he is not. He must therefore know how to manage the image he presents to the outside world and distance himself from any unpopular acts that might render him contemptible in the eyes of the people. The fact that the people are at a distance, removed from the actual practice of politics, means they are not a witness to his actions, and are only able to judge by appearances and results. Their major concern is their material security.

Machiavelli therefore subverts the causal relationship found in Petrarch between the text, the prince and the people. The text, *The Prince*, teaches a new prince how to act to keep power. This will necessitate his acting periodically in a way that is at odds with conventional morality. He must therefore learn how to dissimulate if he is still to maintain the people's respect and admiration. Fear and force should always be in the background, however, as a deterrent. What the people see, as far as events permit, should be a prince who embodies the traditional virtues, but when necessity dictates, the prince should know how to present an image of virtue to the people, how to seem religious, loyal, humane, upright and merciful. They imitate the image not the reality, and the text teaches how to present a semblance of virtue on the mirror's surface which becomes the prince's public face. The prince is aided in this enterprise by the majesty and pomp of the state, which creates the distance between ruler and ruled enabling this policy to work. Those few who actually see what the prince is will realise they have little chance of upsetting an order established by a prince loved by his people.

The problem of Machiavelli's reception is implicit within the text itself. A prince could not be *seen* to accept his advice, a fact that made the formal presentation of such a text an unseemly and potentially embarrassing diplomatic incident.

NOTE ON THE TEXTS

The Italian edition of *The Prince* used for translation is that of
M. Casella (Milan, 1929). The classic critical edition of *Il principe* by L. Burd (Oxford, 1891) is accompanied by an extensive
commentary. The texts of the other political writings are all
translated from the Italian editions published in J.- J. Marchand,
Niccolò Machiavelli: i primi scritti politici (1499–1512) (Padua,
1975). The text of Vettori's letter to Machiavelli of 1513 is taken
from *Opere di Niccolò Machiavelli: Lettere*, vol.3, ed. F. Gaeta
(Turin, 1984), and Machiavelli's reply to Vettori is from N.
Machiavelli, *Tutte le opere*, ed. M. Martelli (Florence 1971).

The Letters of Francesco Vettori and Niccolò Machiavelli:
23 November and 10 December 1513
These letters involve the first mention by Machiavelli to Vettori
of *The Prince* which, he notes in the text, he was still 'enlarging
and polishing'. Machiavelli's letter is a parody of Vettori's,
deliberately contrasting his exclusion from political life with
Vettori's involvement.

How to Deal with the People of the Valdichiana who
have Rebelled
Written between July and early August 1503, this piece is based
on Machiavelli's own involvement in the diplomatic activity
following the rebellion of Arezzo from Florentine rule in June
1502 and its subsequent return, through French intervention, at
the end of August. Cesare Borgia still posed a threat to the
Florentine territorial state at this time.

A Portrait of German Affairs
Based on Machiavelli's missions and contact with the German
court in 1508 and 1509, this tract was the reworking of an

earlier piece (the *Report on German Affairs* of June 1508) and was completed during the second half of 1512.

Duke Valentino's Treacherous Betrayal of Vitellozzo Vitelli, Oliverotto da Fermo and Others

There is no consensus concerning the dating of this piece, although the *terminus ante quem* has been set at the middle of 1517. Some critics locate it almost immediately after the events themselves took place (September 1502–January 1503), whilst conceding that the final version is a reworking of an earlier draft. Although an early and formative experience, therefore, the Borgia episode, as reported here, should be viewed as a more mature work than the other pieces.

The Prince

The traditional dating of *The Prince* is 1513, based on Machiavelli's letter to Vettori above. It has been suggested that the final chapter was added in early 1515 and the text reworked in 1518. The weight of evidence, however, seems to point more convincingly to the traditional dating. Although widely circulated in manuscript form and translated into Latin, the first editions of Machiavelli's *De principatibus* came out in 1532 under the title *Il principe*, being published in both Rome and Florence.

THE PRINCE
AND OTHER POLITICAL WRITINGS

To the worthy gentleman Niccolò Machiavelli, in Florence

My dear friend, I have exercised such sobriety with the pen, as
Cristofano Sernigi says, that I have forgotten where I was with
you. If I remember rightly the last letter I had from you began
with the story of the lion and the wolf.[2] I have looked for it a
little amongst my letters, but since I did not find it quickly I
decided not to look any further for it. For to tell the truth I did
not reply at the time since I suspected that the same thing would
happen to you and me as happened to me and Panzano when
we began playing with cards that were old and worn and sent
for new ones. By the time the person we sent returned with
them, one of us was penniless. In much the same way, we were
speaking of pacifying princes, and they continued to play: so I
was afraid that whilst we were using up letters in pacifying
them, one or other of them might lose his money. And since we
ceased writing, certain things have happened, and although the
party is still not over, things seem to have slowed down a little.
I think it is better not to talk about it until such time as it is
over.

In this letter I have decided to write to you about my life here

---

[1] Francesco Vettori (1474–1539) was elected Florentine ambassador to Rome
on 30 December 1512 in the wake of the Medici's return to Florence. With the
death of Pope Julius II in February 1513, Giovanni de' Medici became Pope Leo
X, extending Medici influence to Rome. Vettori remained ambassador for two
years. Vettori and Machiavelli's friendship was established during the embassy
to the Emperor Maxmilian in 1507.

[2] This refers to Machiavelli's previous letter to Vettori of 26 August 1513,
where he spoke of Aesop's fable of the lion and the wolf, a theme that recurs in
The Prince, Chapter 18.

in Rome. It seems fitting to start by describing where I live, since I have moved and am no longer as near to so many courtesans as I was this summer. My lodgings are in San Michele in Borgo, and are very near the Palazzo and Piazza of San Pietro. It is, however, quite a solitary place since it is near the hill the ancients called the Janiculum. The house itself is very fine and has many rooms, if a little small. It faces the westerly breeze, so the air is perfect.

From the house one can enter the church, which is very useful for me being a religious man, as you know. It is true that the church is used more for walking in than anything else, since neither mass nor any other religious service is ever said there, apart from once a year. From the church one enters a garden which used to be clean and beautiful but is now mostly overgrown, despite there being somebody who regularly goes there to put it in order. From the garden one can climb the Janiculum and wander alone down paths and through vineyards, without being seen by anyone. According to the ancients, the gardens of Nero were set here, and one can see their remains. I have nine servants in this house, and also Brancaccio,[3] a chaplain and a scribe and seven horses, and all my salary is easily spent. When I first arrived here, I started out wanting to live in a lavish and refined manner, inviting foreigners, serving three or four courses, eating from silver and the like. It then occurred to me that I was spending too much and was no better off, so I decided not to invite anybody and live a good ordinary life. I returned the silver to the person who had lent it to me, not only so that I didn't have to take care of it but also because they often asked me to speak to the Pope in relation to some need or other they had. I used to do it, but their needs were not met. So I decided to free myself of this obligation and not trouble or entrust tasks to anybody, so that they wouldn't trouble me.[4]

[3] Giuliano Brancacci features extensively in this correspondence, although it appears that Machiavelli was none too impressed with his ability and trustworthiness.
[4] These comments did not bode well for Machiavelli who would be looking for Vettori to intervene on his behalf in relation to the presentation of *The*

In the morning, with this weather, I get up at about 9.00 a.m., and, when dressed, I go to the Palazzo: not every morning but once every two or three days. There I sometimes speak twenty words with the Pope, ten to the Cardinal de' Medici, and six to the Magnificent Giuliano.[5] If I can't talk to him I speak to Piero Ardinghelli,[6] then to one of the ambassadors that are found in those rooms. In this way I learn some little piece of news, although usually of little import. Once I have done this, I return home, although I periodically dine with the Cardinal de' Medici. Once I am home, I eat with my people, and sometimes one or two outsiders who happen to turn up, for example ser Sano or ser Tommaso who was at Trento, Giovanni Rucellai or Giovanni Girolami.[7] After having eaten I play cards, if there is somebody to play with, and if not I walk through the church and the garden. When the weather is good I also ride a little outside Rome. In the evening I return home, and I have gathered together many history books, especially ones by the Romans, namely Livy, with the summary by Lucio Floro, Sallust, Plutarch, Appian, Cornelius Tacitus, Suetonius, Lampridius and Spartianus, and the others who wrote about the Emperors: Herodian, Ammianus Marcellinus, and Procopius, and I spend time in their company. And I think of the emperors that poor Rome has had to tolerate, a city that previously made the world tremble, and I am not surprised that she has managed to tolerate

Prince and his reintegration into diplomatic life. Vettori's own hopes of securing some benefit from the Pope for himself and his family also met with little success, as he notes elsewhere in his correspondence.

[5] Pope Leo X de' Medici, Cardinal Guilio de' Medici, the future Clement VII, and Giuliano de' Medici, to whom *The Prince* was originally dedicated.

[6] Pietro Ardinghelli was Leo X's personal secretary and a Florentine priest. Machiavelli's reply makes clear his distaste for Ardinghelli as a character.

[7] Ser Sano appears later in the correspondence, his frequent visits to Vettori's house and his known homosexuality causing the ambassador some difficulty. Ser Tommaso must have been on the diplomatic mission they shared in 1507 to the Emperor. Giovanni Rucellai was Pope Leo X's cousin from a prominent Florentine patrician family, and Giovanni Girolami was Cardinal Francesco Soderini's agent at the French court, and known to Machiavelli, who had worked with him when sent to France by Pietro Soderini in June 1510.

popes like the two most recent ones. I write a letter to the Ten[8] once every four days, and tell them some old news of little importance, as I have nothing else to write for the reasons that you yourself understand. I then go to bed after I have eaten and told some little story or other to Brancaccio and to Giovanbatista Nasi who often stays with me. On religious holidays I hear mass, unlike you who periodically skip it. Should you ask me whether I have a courtesan, I reply that I did to begin with, as I wrote to you before. I subsequently stopped, however, fearful of the summer air. Nonetheless I have trained one so that she often comes to see me on her own, and she is reasonably good-looking and pleasant to speak with. Despite the fact that it is solitary, I also have here a next-door neighbour who would not displease you. And although she is of noble family, she's quite obliging.

My dear Niccolò, I invite you to partake of this life. Should you come, it would give me great pleasure, and then we could return to Florence together. Here you wouldn't be obliged to do anything besides walk around observing things, then returning home to chat and laugh. Nor do I want you to think that I live the life of an ambassador, since I always wanted to be free. Sometimes I wear long and sometimes short clothes, I ride alone and walk with my servants, sometimes riding with them. I never go to the House of Cardinals, since there is nobody to visit except the Medici and occasionally Bibbiena,[9] when he is well. People can say what they like, and if I fail to satisfy them they can recall me, for when all is said and done, I want to turn the clock back a year and be in credit, having sold the clothes and the horses, and I don't want to have to spend any of my own money, if at all possible. And I want you to believe this one thing, since I say it without flattery: although I have not worked

---

[8] The Ten, *Dieci di balia*, were the Florentine council of ten citizens responsible for foreign policy.

[9] Bernardo Dovizi da Bibbiena (1470–1520) was a cardinal, agent of Leo X and Papal treasurer. A renowned practical joker, he wrote the comic play *La Calandria* (1512), the most popular renaissance comedy: twenty-six editions between 1521–1600. It was first performed in Urbino in February 1513, and produced by Castiglione, who subsequently included him as one of the interlocutors in his dialogue *The Courtier*.

that hard here, the hustle and bustle is nonetheless so great that one cannot get by without having discussions with many men, and to tell the truth, few of them actually satisfy me, nor have I found a man of better judgement than yourself. 'But the Fates drag us along',[10] for, when I speak at length to certain people, when I read their letters, I am personally shocked that they have reached such positions, positions that consist of nothing but ceremony, lies and fables, there being few who are more than mediocre. Bernardo da Bibbiena, now a cardinal, has a truly subtle intelligence, and is a humorous and discreet person who endured considerable labours in his day. Nonetheless, he is now ill and has been that way for three years, nor am I sure he will ever be what he once was. We often wear ourselves out like this, searching for peace without being successful. In the meantime we should be happy, and what will happen will happen. Remember that I am at your disposal, and that I recommend myself to you, to Filippo and Giovanni Machiavelli, to Donato and messer Ciaio. That is all. May Christ guard over you.

Franciscus Victorius, orator
23 November 1513, Rome

[10] Seneca, *Moral Letters*, 197. Machiavelli takes issue in *The Prince* with this stoical precept of resignation to the whims of the fates. See especially the start of Chapter 25.

LETTER OF NICCOLÒ MACHIAVELLI TO
FRANCESCO VETTORI IN ROME
(10 December 1513)

To his patron and benefactor, the magnificent Florentine orator
Francesco Vettori, in Rome[1]

Magnificent Ambassador. 'Divine favours were never late.'[2] I say
this since it seems to me that I have not so much lost, as mislaid
your favour, as you have not written to me for some time now,
and I was unsure what the reason could be. I paid scant attention
to all the explanations that came to mind, except when I suspected you had ceased writing to me because you had been
notified in writing that I was not a good guardian of your letters.
Yet I knew that with the exception of Filippo and Paulo,[3] I had
not shown them to anybody else. You returned your favour to
me with your most recent letter of the twenty-third of last month,
in which I was most pleased to read how efficiently and calmly
you administer your public office. I recommend you carry on in
the same way, because the person who defers his own interests to
pursue the interests of others, jeopardises his own whilst gaining
no thanks from those he seeks to help. And since Fortune wants
to do everything, she wants to be left alone to do it, for men to

[1] Machiavelli's dependence on Vettori to help him regain office is reflected in
the formality of address to Vettori which contrasts with Vettori's more informal
greeting 'my dear friend'. As Florentine ambassador to the Papal Court, and as
is obvious from the preceding letter, Vettori had access to Pope Leo X de'
Medici and his adherents.
[2] Machiavelli adapts this quotation from Petrarch's *Triumphus Eternitatis*,
line 13.
[3] Filippo Casavecchia was a friend of both correspondents, and may well
have informed Vettori of Machiavelli's project before this letter was sent. That
he had seen the tract is clear from the comments below. Paulo Vettori was
Francesco's younger brother and instrumental in the Medici's return to Florence
in 1512.

stand aside and not give her any trouble, leaving us to await the moment when she eventually allows us to do something. Then will be a good time for you to work harder and keep a closer eye on things, and for me to leave my house in the country and say: 'Here I am.' However, although I would like to honour you in equal measure, I am unable to do anything more in this letter of mine than describe the kind of life I currently lead. If you consider it worth bartering for your own, I will be happy to exchange it.[4]

I am currently in my house in the country, and since my recent setbacks I have not spent more than a total of twenty days in Florence.[5] Until now I have been snaring thrushes with my own hands. I would get up before dawn, prepare the lime, and set out with a bundle of cages on my back, so that I looked like Geta when he returned from the harbour with Amphitryo's books.[6] I used to catch at least two, and at most six, thrushes. I passed the whole of September like this until, to my displeasure, even this pastime, pitiful and strange though it was, was taken from me. As to how I pass my time now, I will tell you. I get up at sunrise and go to a copse of mine that I am having cut down, where I remain for a couple of hours to look over the previous day's work and spend time with the cutters who are always involved in some argument or other, either between themselves or with their neighbours. I could tell you a thousand fine tales about this copse and what has happened to me with both Frosino da Panzano[7] and the others who are after some of the

[4] Machiavelli is referring to the previous letter from Vettori of 23 November, translated above.

[5] Machiavelli is referring to his imprisonment for alleged involvement in the anti-Medicean plot of 1513. He was freed as part of a general amnesty on the election of Giovanni de' Medici as Pope Leo X.

[6] This refers to an incident in the popular story derived from Plautus's play *Amphitruo*, when Geta, a faithful servant who accompanied his master to Greece in search of new knowledge, seeks, on their return, to hand over the books he is carrying to his fellow servant Birria, who had stayed behind with his master's wife. The irony is clear, as Machiavelli is also attempting to persuade Vettori to carry *his* book of new learning to his 'potential' master. See J. Najemy, *Discourses of Power*, in Suggestions for Further Reading.

[7] Frosino da Panzano, also mentioned in Vettori's earlier letter, was obviously a common friend of the two men.

wood. Frosino, in particular, sent for certain bundles of wood without any prior warning and then when it came to paying up wanted to withhold ten lire which he claimed I owed him as a result of his beating me at a game of *cricca* in Antonio Guicciardini's house more than four years previously. I began to raise hell and wanted to denounce the carrier who had come to collect the wood as a thief. Eventually Giovanni Machiavelli intervened and got us to settle our differences. Battista Guicciardini, Filippo Ginori, Tommaso del Bene and certain other citizens each ordered a bundle of wood from me when one of those north winds was blowing. I promised to supply them all, and sent a bundle to Tommaso, which seemed half a bundle by the time it arrived in Florence, as in addition to himself, his wife, boy servant, and children all helped prepare the stack. They reminded me of *el Gabburra* and his boys when they tenderise an ox on Thursdays.[8] Consequently, having seen who was going to profit from it, I informed the others that there wasn't any wood left. They all protested about it, especially Battista who considered it on a par with the misfortunes of Prato.[9]

Leaving the copse behind me, I go to a spring and from there to one of my bird traps. I carry a book with me, either Dante or Petrarch, or one of those minor poets, Tibullus, Ovid, and the like. I read of their amorous passions, and their loves remind me of my own and for a while I revel in those thoughts. I then move down to the road and the inn. I talk with those passing through, asking for news from their villages and learning different things whilst noting the preferences and varied imaginations of men. In the meanwhile the time for lunch arrives, when in the company of my family I eat what produce this poor farm and tiny patrimony provides. Once I have eaten, I return to the inn. The

[8] *El Gabburra* is commonly held to be a butcher. The exact meaning of this phrase is not clear, but it is generally interpreted as referring to the tenderising of a carcass, the comparison being between the beating of the carcass and the beating of the wood into a tight bundle.

[9] Prato was sacked by Spanish forces in August 1512 in an attack famous for its cruelty. Battista Guicciardini was *Podestà*, the chief judicial magistrate of Prato at the time.

innkeeper, a butcher, a miller, and two bakers are usually there. With these men I sink into vulgarity for the whole day playing *cricca* and *tric trac* which give rise to a thousand disputes and endless insults made with hurtful words. More often than not the stake is no more than a *quattrino*, but nonetheless we can be heard shouting from as far away as San Casciano.[10] In this way, surrounded by these lice, I scrape the mould from my brain and give vent to the malice of my fate, being content that she tramples on me along the way, in order to see if she might be ashamed by it.

When evening falls, I return home and enter my study. At the door I take off my everyday clothes, covered in mud and dirt, and put on regal and stately garments. Fittingly attired, I enter the ancient courts of the ancient men, where, being lovingly received by them, I feed on that food which is mine alone, and for which I was born.[11] There, I am not ashamed to speak with them, and ask them the reasons why they acted as they did, and they, because of their humanity, answer me. For four whole hours I feel no boredom, I forget every care, I do not fear poverty, and I am not overawed by death. I lose my self in them. And since Dante says that knowledge is not knowledge unless one retains what one has learned, I have noted down what I found profitable in their conversation and composed a little book *De principatibus*, in which I immerse myself as deeply as I can in thoughts on the subject, arguing what a principality is, what types there are, how they are acquired and how retained, and why they are lost.[12] If any of my caprices ever pleased you,

[10] Machiavelli is describing the hostelry of Sant'Andrea in Percussina, in the Val di Pesa just outside Florence, which is still standing. The village of San Casciano is some three miles along the same road. The games he describes are a mixture of card games and backgammon.

[11] The contrast is between the spiritual sustenance he receives in the company of the ancients and the paltry fare he consumes with his family, as mentioned above.

[12] The Latin title means '*On principalities*'. Machiavelli twice refers to the work in his *Discourses*, once as *il nostro trattato del Principati* (II, i), and once as *il nostro trattato del Principe* (III, 42). The first printed editions in 1532 carried the title *The Prince*. The reference to Dante relates to *The Divine Comedy, Paradiso*, V, 41–2.

this one should not displease you; and it ought to be pleasing to a prince, and most of all to a new prince. For this reason I am addressing it to his Magnificence Giuliano.[13] Filippo Casavecchia has seen it. He will be able to inform you in part concerning the work itself, and of the discussions I had with him, although I am constantly enlarging and revising it.

You would have me leave this life, Magnificent Ambassador, to come and enjoy yours with you. I will certainly do it, but what holds me back at present are certain personal matters that will be cleared up within six weeks. The fact that the Soderini are in Rome also makes me hesitate, as, if I go there, I will be forced to visit them and talk with them. I am fearful that on my return I might expect to dismount not at my house, but rather at the Bargello, because although this government has very strong foundations and is very secure, it is nevertheless new and consequently suspicious.[14] Nor is there a lack of smart-Alecs who, in order to appear like Paulo Bertini,[15] would feed others information and leave me to pay the price. I ask you to alleviate this fear, and then I will certainly come to see you within the time stated above.

I have discussed my little tract with Filippo, and whether it was a good idea to present it or not, and being a good idea, whether I should take it there myself or send it. In not presenting it, my fear is that it might not be read by Giuliano, but by

[13] Giulano de' Medici (1479–1516) was the third son of Lorenzo *il Magnifico* de' Medici, and on the return of the Medici to Florence in 1512 he was the most authoritative member of the family after his brother Giovanni, Pope Leo X. On Giuliano's death in 1516, Machiavelli dedicated the work to Lorenzo, Giuliano's and Giovanni's nephew, who was rumoured to be seeking the duchy of Urbino, the setting of another classic Renaissance handbook, Castiglione's *The Book of the Courtier* of 1528.

[14] Machiavelli is naturally afraid of being seen to consort with his former patron, Piero Soderini, who as the ex-leader of the Florentine Republic had been sentenced to five years in Ragusa, although this condition of residence was varied shortly afterwards, allowing him to reside in Rome with his brother Cardinal Francesco Soderini. The Bargello was the headquarters of the Florentine judicial police, the home of the city's prison and the place were Machiavelli was put on the rack earlier in the year, on suspicion of plotting against the newly returned Medici.

[15] Paulo Bertini is yet to be identified, but the slur is clear.

others, and that this Ardinghelli character might derive honour from this latest effort of mine.[16] The necessity that drives me on, forces me to present it to him, because I am wearing myself down and cannot carry on like this for much longer without becoming despised because of my poverty. In addition there is the desire that these Medici lords should begin to make use of me, even if they should begin by making me roll a stone, because then, should I fail to win their favour, I could only blame myself.[17] And through this work, should it be read, they would realise that the fifteen years I have been studying the art of government have not been passed in sleep and games. Anyone should consider it an honour to be served by someone who has gained so much experience which has been paid for by others. Nor should they doubt my loyalty, because, having always kept my faith, I do not intend to learn to break it now. A person who has remained loyal and honest for forty-three years, as I have, should not be able to change his character. My poverty bears witness to my fidelity and honesty.

I would desire, therefore, that you write to me again concerning your views on this matter, and I commend myself to you. May you be happy.

10 December 1513
Niccolò Machiavelli in Florence

[16] Machiavelli is reacting to Vettori's remarks in the previous letter about spending time with Pietro Ardinghelli in Rome. There was little love lost between the two men, and later in August 1515 Ardinghelli recommended that Giuliano de' Medici keep Machiavelli from holding any civic office in Florence.

[17] The reference is to the labour of Sisyphus in Hades, that of fulfilling an impossible task. He had to set a rock on the top of a hill, but every time he reached the summit, the rock inevitably rolled back down.

HOW TO DEAL WITH THE PEOPLE OF THE
VALDICHIANA WHO HAVE REBELLED
(*Del modo di trattare i popoli della valdichiana ribellati*)

{When Lucius Furius Camillus returned to Rome after conquering the people of Latium, who have rebelled against the Romans on several occasions, he entered the Senate and made proposals}[1] concerning what should be done with the Latin towns and cities. The words that he used, taken almost verbatim from Livy and the Senate's judgement were as follows:[2]

Conscript fathers, what needed to be done by warfare and weapons in Latium has been successfully completed, through the goodwill of the gods and the strength [*virtù*] of our soldiers. The enemy's armies lie dead near Preda and Astura, and all the cities and towns of Latium and Antium, the city of the Volsci, have been captured either by force or surrender. It now remains for us to discuss how we can secure ourselves against them in the future, whether by treating them severely, or by freely forgiving them, since they often rebel and place us in danger. The gods have given you the power to decide whether Latium should continue to stand or not, and allowed you the chance to secure yourselves against them for ever. Consider, therefore, whether you want to punish severely those who have given themselves over to you, and whether you want to destroy Latium totally, reducing a territory which furnished you with auxiliary troops when you were in danger, to

[1] This manuscript is not in Machiavelli's hand, but has come down to us via a sixteenth-century copy by Giuliano de' Ricci. The sections in brackets { } are hypothetical reconstructions by Ricci of the missing sections of the text.

[2] Livy, *Ab Urbe Condita*, VIII, 13, 11–14.8. Rome completed her conquest of the rebellious Latins in 338 BC, after which she embarked on a national phase of conquest. The speech cited comes at a significant point of Livy's overall narrative, the moment where the Romans have to decide whether to rule by kindness or terror. Their subsequent power was based on their answer to this question. It is not surprising, therefore, to find Machiavelli adopting this belief so enthusiastically, both here and in *The Prince*, Chapter 5.

a desolate place, and whether, following in your forefathers' footsteps, you want to augment the Roman republic by bringing those you have vanquished to live in Rome. The chance to enhance the city's glory has thus been presented to you. All I have to say to you is this: that the power which has loyal subjects who hold their ruler in affection is the most stable power. What has to be discussed must be discussed quickly, since you are keeping so many people suspended between hope and fear, people whose uncertainty needs to be resolved either by punishing them or rewarding them. My duty was to ensure that the judgement was yours, a duty which has been fulfilled. It is now your task to discuss what is most suitable and profitable for the Republic.

The leaders of the Senate praised the consul's report, but because there were different reasons for what happened in each town and city, they said that they could not discuss the matter in general terms, but would rather consider each case individually. When the consul had outlined each city's particular case, the senators decided that the Lanuvini should become Roman citizens, and that the religious objects seized from them during the war should be returned. They also granted citizenship to the Aricini, Nomentani and the Pedani. The Tusculani were allowed to retain their privileges, and the responsibility for the rebellion was blamed on a few of the most suspect citizens. The Veliterni, however, were cruelly put down as they were long-standing Roman citizens, and had rebelled on numerous occasions. Consequently, their city was destroyed and all its citizens sent to live in Rome. Antium was sent new obedient citizens to secure it, and all their ships were taken from them and a law promulgated which prevented them from building new ones.

One can see from these decisions that when the Romans had to judge these rebellious cities of theirs, they thought it necessary either to gain their loyalty with favours or deal with them in such a way that they would never have to worry about them again. Any policy that stood between these two courses of action was thus considered dangerous. When they subsequently came to pass judgement, therefore, they used either one or the other policy, distributing favours where there was the possibility of reconciliation, and treating the others, whom they considered beyond hope, in such a way that they could never harm them again. The Romans had two ways of enforcing the second policy. The first involved ruining the cities and sending the inhabitants to live in Rome, the second in clearing the cities of old inhabitants and sending new ones there, or leaving the old ones there but sending so many new ones that the old ones could never conspire or decide anything against the wishes of the Senate. These two methods of securing themselves were adhered to in the above judgement, as they destroyed the Velitrae and sent new inhabitants to Antium.

I have heard it said that histories are the instructors of how to act, and especially for princes, and that the world has always been inhabited in the same way by men who have had the same passions, and that there have always been those who have served and those who command, some serving against their will and others willingly, and some even rebelling and being recaptured. Should anyone doubt this, let them reflect on the case of Arezzo over the past year, indeed on all the cities of Valdichiana. What they have done is very similar to what the Latin people did. Their rebellion and subsequent recapture was the same as the current one, although there are considerable differences in the way they rebelled and were retaken. Nonetheless, the rebellion and re-acquisition are similar.[3]

If, therefore, it is true that histories are the instructors of how to act, it would not have been a bad idea for those who had to punish and judge the cities of the Valdichiana to follow the example of and imitate those who were rulers of the world, especially in a case where they give exact instruction about how to proceed. For just as they reached different decisions because of the people's different crimes, so should you when you find

---

[3] Arezzo and the smaller towns in the valley region known as the Valdichiana had rebelled against Florence in June 1502. Florence suspected the involvement of Cesare Borgia, and had information from captured spies that Vitellozzo Vitelli and the exiled Piero de' Medici were involved. As Secretary to the Second Chancery, Machiavelli himself had been involved in the diplomatic dealings to pacify the region.

your rebels have committed different crimes. If you should say: 'We have done it already', I would answer that it has been partially done, but that the best and most important part has been missed. I think it was a good decision that the *Capitoli* were maintained in Cortona, Castiglione, Borgo Sansepolcro and Foiano, and that you have sought to win them over with gifts, as I consider them similar to the Lanuvini, Aricini, Nomentani, Tusculani and Pedani, who were judged the same way by the Romans.[4] But I really do not approve that the Aretines, who are comparable to the Veliterni and Antiani, have not been treated like them. If the Romans' judgement is worthy of commendation, your judgement deserves to be censured in equal measure. The Romans thought that rebellious peoples should either be given gifts or extinguished once and for all, and that every other course was very dangerous. It does not seem to me that you have done either of these things to the Aretines. For compelling them to come to Florence every day when you have deprived them of their offices, sold their possessions and berated them in public for having kept soldiers in their houses, does not constitute granting them favours. Similarly, leaving their walls standing, letting five-sixths of the population remain there, and not sending other people to live there to suppress them, does not constitute securing yourself against them. Nor, as regards the Aretines, does it involve being organised so that you might have to pay out more on them than on defending yourself against an enemy who might attack you. The experience of 1498 proved that although Arezzo had not yet rebelled, and was not as hostile towards your city, nonetheless, when the Venetian troops entered Bibbiena, you had to deploy the Duke of Milan's troops and Count Rinuccio with his company to hold it firm. If there had been no suspicion, you could have used these troops against your enemies in the Casentino, and it would not have been necessary to take Paulo Vitelli away from Pisa to send him to the Casentino

---

[4] The *Capitoli* were a series of headings and statutes drawn up by Florence commissioners sent to these subject towns to pacify them; they stipulated the penalties for breaking the peace.

instead.[5] Things were made more dangerous for you as a consequence of being forced to declare your lack of trust in them, and more expensive than if they had been loyal. Bearing in mind, therefore, the state of things now, the way things stood before, and the way the Aretines are currently being held, if you were attacked – may God forbid – it could safely be assumed that either Arezzo would rebel or its defence would prove so difficult that the cost to the city would be intolerable.

I also want to consider the following questions: whether or not you could be attacked at the present time, and whether there are those who have designs on Arezzo, for I have heard such things being discussed. {Let us leave aside a discussion of those fears that you might have of the princes over the Alps, and instead discuss} the fear that is closer to home. Anyone who has observed Duke Valentino will notice that, as regards holding on to the states he already possesses, he has never sought to rely too much on Italian allies, having always had little respect for the Venetians and even less for you. If this is true, it means that he is planning to acquire sufficient power in Italy to make himself secure on his own terms, and can then choose at will which powerful ruler he wishes to have as an ally. The question remains whether this is his intention, and whether he does aspire to rule over Tuscany, as the nearest and most fitting territory to combine with his other states to form a kingdom. That this is actually his plan is obvious when you consider the combination of the reasons stated above, his ambition, his reluctance to ratify an agreement with you and his persistent refusal to come to any conclusions with you about anything. It now remains {to be seen} whether the time is ripe for the execution of his plans. I remember Cardinal Soderini[6] being told that one of the attri-

[5] Paulo Vitelli was a mercenary leader hired by the Florentines in June 1498, and brother of Vitellozzo Vitelli. When the Venetians attacked Tuscany in September 1498, invading the Casentino and Mugello, Paulo was transferred from Pisa to hold them off. The Florentines eventually killed Vitelli for treason in October 1499 due to his unsatisfactory conduct of the siege against Pisa.

[6] Cardinal Francesco Soderini (1453–1524) was the brother of the then leader of Florence, Piero Soderini (1451–1522), and was accompanied by Machiavelli on his embassy to Cesare Borgia in Urbino in late June 1503.

butes of great men that could be attributed to the Pope and the Duke was this: that they are shrewd opportunists and know how to use the main chance well, an opinion that is proved by the evidence of what they have achieved when given the opportunity. If one has to discuss whether now is an opportune and safe moment for the Duke to attack you, I would say it was not. Considering, however, that the Duke cannot wait for the perfect moment, as he has little time remaining due to the Pope being not long for this world,[7] it is necessary that he takes the first opportunity that is offered him, and that, for the most part, he entrusts his cause to fortune.

[7] Pope Alexander VI, Cesare Borgia's father, died in mid August 1503, just after the composition of this tract. That this proved a crucial turning point in Borgia's fortunes is noted by Machiavelli in Chapter 7 of *The Prince*.

A PORTRAIT OF GERMAN AFFAIRS[1]
(*Ritratto delle cose della Magna*)

Nobody can doubt the power of Germany, since it abounds in men, riches and arms. As regards riches, there is not a single city-state that does not have a public surplus, and it is commonly believed that Strasbourg alone has several million florins. This is because they do not spend more than the costs they incur in meeting the expenses of keeping their supplies at a healthy level, for once they have made the initial outlay, the cost of maintaining them is small. This is a most excellent custom of theirs, since they always have enough in the public realm to eat, drink and provide fuel for a year, and can also, by working their trades, feed the people and manual workers at a time of siege for a whole year without incurring any loss. They spend nothing on soldiers, as they keep their own men armed and drilled. On feast-days, instead of games, some men practise with the musket or with the pike, others with weapons of one kind and another, and they challenge each other's honour and play similar enjoyable games amongst themselves. They spend little on salaries and other things, and consequently each city-state finds its public purse full.[2]

---

[1] Machiavelli's knowledge of Germany was gained during his first legation to the Tyrol between January and June 1508, and his second legation to the Imperial court based in Mantua in November and December 1509. As a result of the first legation he wrote a brief *Report on German Affairs* which provided the basis of this later piece, although additional information concerning military matters was added subsequent to the second legation and his observation of the wars between 1509–12. Machiavelli generalised from these limited experiences of the Tyrol and conflated Swiss features with German characteristics.

[2] Machiavelli's idealised view of the Germans as a spendthrift, primitive and hardy people is partly a critique of what he sees as an effeminate and corrupt Italy and, it has been suggested, is partially derived from the Tacitean myth of the *Germania*. He also insists that Germany's strength is derived from their

The people are rich as private individuals for the following reasons: they live like poor people, they do not build, or spend money on clothes and have no furnishings in their houses. All they require is a plentiful supply of bread and meat, and a stove to keep them warm when it gets cold. Those who do not have these things go without, and do not try to acquire them. In ten years, they spend about two florins on themselves, and everybody lives according to their station and nobody remarks on what they lack, but rather on what they need. Their necessities are a lot less than ours. The upshot of these customs is that very little money leaves their country, as they are content with those things which are produced in their own country. Money constantly enters, and is brought into, their country by people who desire their hand-made goods, a trade indulged in by almost all Italians. The profits are increased due to the benefits that result from working and making things manually, for it requires little expenditure on other materials. In this way they enjoy their primitive lifestyle and their freedom, and are consequently reluctant to engage in warfare unless they are paid more than usual, and even this would be insufficient if they were not compelled by their city-states. Consequently, an Emperor requires much more money than any other prince, since the better the condition of the men, the more reluctant they are to enter wars.

As things currently stand, the city-states either join with the princes to support the campaigns of the Emperor, or, because they are sufficiently strong, they carry them out themselves.[3] But neither of them would favour an increase in the Emperor's power, for, in the past, whenever he has been a powerful

citizen militias, in contrast to the excessive use of mercenary soldiers in Italy. See *The Prince*, Chapters 10 and 26.

[3] Machiavelli is here conflating German and Swiss states and princes, Switzerland being a part of the Holy Roman Empire. Switzerland itself was divided into thirteen cantons to which were allied numerous smaller republics. They were famed for their military prowess on account of their resistance to Charles the Bold, Duke of Burgundy, between 1476–7. Maximilian was attempting to unify the disparate elements within a politically fragmented Empire in the interests of the Habsburgs, but was opposed by the German patriots.

landowner, he would dominate and belittle the princes and reduce them to a state of obedience whereby he could use them when it suited him and not when it suited them. The King of France currently acts like this, as did King Louis before him, as he reduced them to a state of obedience which is still observed today, through the use of arms and the odd assassination.

The same thing used to happen to the city-states, for the Emperor would seek to reduce their power so that he could manage them as he wished, and take whatever he wanted from them, rather than what they saw fit to give him. But the reason for the disunion between the city-states and the princes is understood to lie in the many conflicting groups that there are in that land. Focusing specifically on two general divisions, they say that the Germans consider all the Swiss as enemies, and all the princes are considered enemies by the Emperor. It maybe seems strange to hear that the Swiss and the city-states are enemies, as each strives to the same end – that of saving their liberty and guarding themselves against the princes. But their disunion results from the fact that the Swiss are not only enemies of both the princes and the city-states but are also enemies of the landed nobles. In their country neither of these two groups exists, and they enjoy a true freedom without any differentiation between men, apart from that which results from holding public office. The Swiss example makes the remaining landed nobles in the city-states fearful, and all of their efforts go into keeping the Swiss and the city-states divided and on unfriendly terms with each other.

All the military men of the city-states consider the Swiss as enemies, and are animated by a natural jealousy which results from their perception that they are less esteemed militarily than the Swiss. Consequently, it is impossible to mix the two together in the same camp, in either small or large numbers, without fights breaking out.

There is no need for any further discussion concerning the animosity of the princes towards both the city-states and the Swiss, since it is well known, as is the animosity between the Emperor and the princes. One has to understand that in viewing the princes as his main enemy, and in not being able to weaken their power on his own, the Emperor has used the support of the city-states, and, for the very same reason, has also periodically negotiated with the Swiss, whose confidence he seemed to have gained some time ago. Consequently, when all these divisions are simultaneously considered, and the divisions that exist between princes themselves and between different city-states are added, it becomes difficult for the Emperor to establish the kind of union that he needs in the Empire. Whoever thinks campaigns against Germany are brave and easily launched should bear in mind that there is no prince in Germany who is able, or who dares, to oppose the Emperor's schemes in the way they used to in the distant past. Nevertheless, do not think that the princes' lack of help is much of an impediment to the Emperor's plans, since those who do not dare declare war on him are brave enough to deny him help, and those who are not brave enough to deny him help are sufficiently courageous to ignore the promises of help that they make to him. Those who do not even dare to do this, dare to defer their promises to such an extent that they are not in time to be of any use. All these considerations impede and upset any plans. The truth of this was demonstrated when the Emperor first wanted to descend into Italy against the wishes of the Venetians and the French, for the city-states of Germany promised him nineteen thousand infantry and three thousand horses at the Diet of Constance held at that time, and yet he was never able to put together more than a total number of five thousand.[4] This happened because when the men of one city-state arrived, the others departed having finished their stint, and some city-states sent money instead of men. And because this happened frequently, and bearing in mind all the other different reasons, the troops never mustered together and the enterprise ended badly.

[4] The Diet of Constance, called by the Emperor Maximilian, was held in August 1507, with the aim of raising an army to help enter northern Italy and re-establish Imperial authority, and have Maximilian crowned Holy Roman Emperor. He was granted the right to call himself Emperor elect by Pope Julius II, but he never actually succeeded in being crowned by the Pope.

It is well established that the strength of Germany lies considerably more in its city-states than in its princes, since its princes are of two kinds, either temporal or spiritual. The temporal ones have become almost impotent, partly through their own fault (as every principality is divided between several princes as a consequence of the equal division of estates that they observe) and partly through having diminished the power of the Emperor with the help of the city-states, as noted above. Consequently, they have become useless as allies.

There are also, as noted above, ecclesiastical princes who, if not annihilated by the hereditary divisions, have been weakened by both the ambition of their city-states and the backing of the Emperor, so that the voting Archbishops and their like are unable to achieve anything in their own large city-states. Consequently, it comes about that neither they, nor their towns, can back the Emperor's campaigns when they really want to, because they are divided against each other.

But let us turn to the Frankish and Imperial city-states which are the backbone of that land and have both money and order. They are lukewarm in providing support for the Emperor for a variety of reasons, given that their principal aim is to maintain their liberty rather than acquire power, and that they do not care that others possess things that they themselves do not desire. Consequently, as they are numerous and their own masters, when they do decide to provide military support, their help is belated and not as useful as it might be. The following serves as an example. Not many years ago, the Swiss assaulted the state of Maximilian and Swabia. His majesty came to an agreement with these city-states to subdue the Swiss, and they committed themselves to keeping fourteen thousand men in the field. But there was never more than half that number there at any one time, because, when men from one city-state arrived, the others departed, so that the Emperor, despairing of the campaign, came to an agreement with the Swiss and handed over to them the city of Basle. Now if they adopted such policies in their own campaigns, you can imagine what they might do in other people's campaigns. The cumulative result of all these things is that they diminish their own power, and it becomes practically useless to the Emperor. The Venetians, because of the commerce they have with the merchants of the German city-states, have understood this better than anyone, and have always remained deferential in all their dealings and discussions with the Emperor. If they had been afraid of his power they would have made some sort of arrangement, either with money or by ceding territory. But whenever it seemed likely that his power might be united, they did not seek to prevent it, because they knew there was no chance of its actually happening, and consequently they were sufficiently bold to take the risk. And anyway, if commonly held things are fought over so fiercely in a city, the same thing is even more likely to happen in a country.

The city-states, therefore, realise that any acquisitions that are made in Italy or elsewhere would be for the princes' benefit rather than theirs, as the princes would be able to profit personally: something that it is impossible for a city-state to do. Where the reward is necessarily unequal, men are unwilling to spend equally. And although the power of the city-states is great, they are not in a position to profit from it. Anyone who is afraid of their power should consider the things mentioned above, and the effects that this power has had over many years, and they would see the extent of the foundations that could be constructed there.

Although they are a little heavy, the German cavalry are quite well mounted, and also physically well armed in the areas they traditionally arm. But it is also worth noting that they would not pass muster in a military encounter against the Italians or French. This is not on account of the quality of their men, but because they wear no armour at all on horseback, and have small saddles which are weak and without saddle bows. As a result the slightest blow throws them to the ground. They are also weakened by the lack of any armour worn below the torso to protect the thighs and legs. Consequently, unable to withstand the all-important first blow, both the infantry and the cavalry are unable to fight at close quarters, as they can be injured in the unprotected areas I mentioned above. Every foot soldier with a pike is then capable of either unsaddling, or disembowelling them. They are also unable to control their horses well, because the weight of the riders unsettles them.

The infantry are excellent and the men have fine physiques. This contrasts with the Swiss who are small, unkempt and unpleasant characters. They arm themselves lightly, with little more than a pike or a knife in order to be more flexible, speedy and mobile. They claim that they arm themselves like this because no breastplate, corslet or cuirass would defend them from the only enemy they do have, namely the artillery.

They have no fear of other weapons, since they say that they keep their formation so tightly that it is impossible to enter their ranks, or get within a pike's length of them.

They are excellent soldiers in the open field of battle, but useless at storming towns and not much better at defending them. They are generally of no use when they are unable to assume the formations that they use in their own militias. The experience they underwent in Italy proves this, especially when they had to storm towns, as happened in Padua and elsewhere, where they performed badly.[5] When they were in open battle, on the other hand, they did well. Indeed, if the French had not had lansquenets at the day of the Battle of Ravenna between the French and the Spanish, they would have lost. For whilst both sets of infantry were in close combat, the Spanish had already broken the French and Gascon infantry who would all have been killed and captured if the Alamanni and their forces had not come to their aid.[6] And so one can see that when the

---

[5] Padua was besieged by Imperial forces in September 1509.

[6] The Battle of Ravenna between French forces and the Holy League took place on 11 April 1512, proving inconclusive. Florence stood alone in supporting the French, and celebrated the apparent French victory, aided by Florentine troops like the Alamanni mercenaries. However, it turned out to be a hollow victory, with the French commander de Foix being killed in the final phases of battle and the League forces retreating intact. France was under the dual threat of invasion by the English and attack from the Swiss, and therefore gradually withdrew from Italy leaving Florence isolated and at the mercy of the League forces. The result was the return of the Medici to Florence.

Catholic King recently declared war on the French in Guienne, the Spanish troops were more afraid of a group of Alamanni under the most Christian King than they were of all the other infantry, and they avoided the chance of entering into hand-to-hand combat with them.[7]

[7] In May of 1512 King Ferdinand atacked Guienne across the Pyrenees. The 'most Christian King' was Louis XII (1462–1515), King of France, and the 'Catholic King' King Ferdinand II of Spain (1452–1516).

DUKE VALENTINO'S TREACHEROUS BETRAYAL
OF VITELLOZZO VITELLI, OLIVEROTTO DA FERMO
AND OTHERS
(Il tradimento del Duca Valentino al Vitellozzo Vitelli,
Oliverotto da Fermo et altri)

Duke Valentino returned from Lombardy, where he had gone to justify himself to King Louis of France in the light of numerous accusations made against him by the Florentines as a result of the rebellion of Arezzo and the other towns of the Valdichiana, and went straight to Imola.[1] He was planning to stay with his troops there, and launch a campaign against Messer Giovanni Bentivoglio, tyrant of Bologna, as he wanted to reduce that city to his rule and make it the capital of his dukedom of the Romagna. Once the Vitelli and Orsini and their other followers understood this, they considered that the Duke was becoming too powerful and that they had reason to fear that once he had taken Bologna he might seek to eliminate them, in order to remain the only armed force in Italy. They organised a meeting on the subject at Magione, in the territory of Perugia, where the Cardinal, Paulo, and the Duke of Gravina Orsini, Vitellozzo Vitelli, Oliverotto da Fermo, Giampagolo Baglioni, despot of Perugia, and Messer Antonio da Venafro, who represented Pandolfo Petrucci, ruler of Siena, gathered together.[2] There they discussed the Duke's power and his intentions, and

[1] Machiavelli's first contact with Cesare Borgia was in June 1502 when he accompanied Francesco Soderini, Bishop of Volterra, on a diplomatic mission to meet the Duke. In a spectacular coup Borgia had seized the duchy of Urbino the day before their arrival, a move that impressed Machiavelli who noted Borgia's prudent and speedy execution of his strategy. The rebellion of Arezzo and the Valdichiana against Florentine rule in the summer of 1502 was discussed by Machiavelli in a piece of 1503, *How to Deal with the People of the Valdichiana who have Rebelled,* in which he mentions Borgia's remarks concerning the importance of seizing the main chance and using it well. See above.

[2] These men represented an alliance of already deposed leaders, those who feared Borgia's rapid expansion, and Borgia's own former mercenary commanders. Antonio da Venafro is also mentioned in *The Prince,* Chapter 22.

how it was necessary for them to bridle his appetite before they too ran the risk of being ruined together with the others. Accordingly, they decided not to abandon the Bentivogli and to seek to win over the Florentines, sending their men to both places, with promises of help to the former and petitions to the latter, urging them to join together against the common enemy.

News of this meeting immediately spread throughout Italy, and those peoples who were discontented under the Duke's rule, including the people of Urbino,[3] took hope in the possibility of being able to stir things up. As a result, whilst minds were still undecided, some citizens of Urbino planned to seize the fortress of San Leo which was occupied by the Duke's supporters. They took the opportunity presented by the following circumstances. The castellan was strengthening the fortress and, having ordered timbers to be brought there, the conspirators arranged that some beams that were being dragged into the fortress should be left over the drawbridge in such a way that, being blocked, it could not be raised by those inside. Seizing this opportunity, the armed conspirators rushed the bridge and then the fortress. Consequently, as soon as this seizure became known, the whole state rebelled and recalled the former Duke, having been encouraged not so much by the seizure of the fortress as by the meeting at Magione, which they thought would support them.

When they learnt of the rebellion of Urbino, those at the meeting considered that the opportunity was not to be spurned and, joining forces, they advanced to seize those towns that still remained in the Duke's hands. Once again they sent to Florence to entreat that republic to join them in putting out this fire that threatened them both, demonstrating how the enterprise was as good as won and the opportunity second to none. But the Florentines, on account of the hatred they bore towards the Vitelli and Orsini for various reasons, not only refused to join them, but also sent Niccolò Machiavelli, their secretary, to offer

---

[3] Urbino had been seized by Valentino earlier in 1502, deposing Duke Guidobaldo da Montefeltro whose rule was later immortalised in Castiglione's *The Book of the Courtier* of 1528.

the Duke shelter and aid against these new enemies of his.[4] He
found the Duke at Imola, and afraid, as in one fell swoop, and
totally unexpectedly, he found himself on the brink of war,
unarmed and with his own troops turned hostile. Once the Duke
had regained his courage on the news of the Florentine offer, he
cunningly sought to stall the war with the few troops he still
possessed, and with peace negotiations, whilst at the same time
gathering help. This he did in two ways: firstly by requesting
troops from the King of France, and secondly by hiring all the
mercenaries and anybody else who made their living on horseback in some way, and giving them all money.

Despite this, the enemy advanced and headed towards Fos-
sombrone where some of the Duke's forces had struck camp.
These were routed by the Vitelli and Orsini. This news forced
the Duke to direct all his efforts to seeing if he could put a stop
to this defiant mood with peace negotiations. As he was a very
accomplished fraud, he did not waste any opportunity in giving
them to understand that they had moved their forces against a
man whose intention was to hand over to them what he had
acquired, and that he wished the princedom to be theirs. The
title of prince was all he wanted. He was so successful in
persuading them that they sent Lord Paulo [Orsini] to the Duke
to negotiate a truce and halted their troops. But the Duke did
not halt his own military preparations, and with great speed he
built up a body of cavalry and infantry. In order that these
preparations should go undetected, he distributed the troops in
small groups throughout the Romagna.

In the meantime another five hundred French lances arrived,
and although he was already sufficiently strong to be able to
avenge himself against his enemies in open warfare, he nevertheless considered that to deceive them would be a safer and more
profitable course of action, and for this reason he continued the

---

[4] Machiavelli spent nearly three and a half months with Borgia between
October 1502 and January 1503, during which time he sent regular reports to
the Florentine councils. He wrote the current tract as a result of this first-hand
experience, and used it as a basis for his observations in the text of *The Prince*,
notably Chapter 7.

peace negotiations. He took such pains over the matter that a peace was eventually signed with them, in which he confirmed their former military contracts, gave them four thousand ducats as a gift, promised not to attack the Bentivogli, and formed a tie of kinship with messer Giovanni. He also gave up his right to be able to order them into his presence more than they considered fitting. For their part, they promised to restore the duchy of Urbino to him, together with all the other territory they had taken, to assist him in all his military enterprises and not to declare war on anyone or sign military contracts with anybody without his express licence.

After this agreement was signed, Guidobaldo, Duke of Urbino, again took flight and returned to Venice, having first destroyed all the fortresses in the region. For, placing his trust in the people, he did not want the enemy to occupy those fortresses that he knew he was unable to defend and, using them, hold his supporters in check.[5] Duke Valentino, on the other hand, once he had signed this accord, departed from Imola at the beginning of November and went to Cesena, together with the French troops, having scattered his own forces throughout the Romagna. He remained there for many days, discussing with the representatives of the Vitelli and Orsini who were stationed with their troops in Urbino, what new undertaking they should embark upon. As they failed to decide on any particular policy, Liverotto da Fermo was sent with the offer that if the Duke wanted to launch a campaign against Tuscany they were in favour, if not, they would go ahead with the storming of Senigallia. To this the Duke replied that he was unwilling to start a war in Tuscany on account of his friendship with the Florentines, but that he was more than happy that they should proceed against Senigallia.

As a result, therefore, he was notified after only a few days that the town had surrendered to them, but that the fortress had not agreed to the surrender as the castellan wished to hand it

[5] Duke Guidobaldo destroyed the fortresses of Gubbio and Pergola. See *The Prince*, Chapter 20.

over to the Duke in person and not to anyone else, and so they pleaded with him to come to the city. The opportunity seemed ripe to the Duke as it would not arouse any suspicion, for he was being summoned by them and not going there on his own account. In order to reassure them further, he dismissed all the French troops who, with the exception of a hundred lances belonging to Monsignor di Ciandales, his brother-in-law, returned to Lombardy. Leaving Cesena in mid December, he went to Fano, where with all the guile and wisdom he possessed he persuaded the Vitelli and Orsini to await him at Senigallia, pointing out to them that remaining distant would not render their accord trustworthy or durable, and that he was a man who liked to make use of the troops and advice of his friends. And although Vitellozzo remained somewhat reluctant, as his brother's death had taught him that one should not injure a Prince and then trust him, he nevertheless agreed to wait for him, having been persuaded by Paulo Orsini who had been corrupted by the Duke with promises and gifts.

So on the evening before he was due to leave Fano (namely 30 December 1502), the Duke revealed his plan to eight of his most trusted men, amongst whom were Don Michele and Monsignor d'Elna,[6] who later became cardinal, and he ordered that as soon as Vitellozzo, Paulo Orsini, the Duke of Gravina and Oliverotto had come to meet him they should form pairs and stand either side of one of the above mentioned men, the Duke assigning particular men to each of the four. They would then be accompanied into Senigallia in this formation, and the men were not to permit them to break rank until they had arrived at their lodgings and had been seized. He also ordered that all his forces, both on horse and foot, totalling some two thousand cavalry and ten thousand infantry in all, should gather at dawn the next morning by the River Metaurus, five miles from Fano, and await his arrival in person.

So, on the last day of December he found himself on the

---

[6] Monsignor d'Elna, Francesco de Loris, was secretary to Pope Alexander VI and was made a cardinal in May 1503.

banks of the Metaurus with these troops and he ordered five hundred cavalry to ride in advance followed by all the infantry and then himself and the remainder of his forces.

Fano and Senigallia are two cities in the Marches which stand on the Adriatic coast, about fifteen miles apart, in such a way that as one goes towards Senigallia the mountains stand on the right-hand side. The base of these mountains periodically approaches the shore, so that there is very little space between them and the sea, and even where the gap is wider it never exceeds more than two miles. The city of Senigallia is little more than an archer's shot from the foot of these mountains and less than a mile from the port. Alongside it runs a small river which washes against the part of the city walls that faces toward Fano. The road, until it approaches Senigallia itself, runs for long stretches alongside the mountains. Once it arrives at the river that passes by Senigallia, it turns to the left and follows the river bank for about the length of an archer's shot until it arrives at a bridge which crosses the river and almost joins the gate that leads into Senigallia, not as the crow flies, but diagonally. In front of the gate is a cluster of houses with a square, one side of which is formed by the bank of the river.

Once the Vitelli and Orsini had decided to await the Duke and honour him personally, they withdrew their troops to some castles about six miles from Senigallia in order to make room for his troops. Only Liverotto was left in Senigallia together with his followers who numbered a thousand infantry and one hundred and fifty cavalry, and were lodged in the group of houses mentioned above.

With the situation as described, the Duke Valentino approached Senigallia, and when the first group of cavalry arrived at the bridge, they did not cross, but stopped there. Some of the horses turned their hindquarters towards the river and others towards the country, leaving a path through the middle for the infantry, who marched down it and entered the town without stopping. Vitellozzo, Paulo and the Duke of Gravina, riding mules, went to meet the Duke accompanied by a few cavalry. Vitellozzo, unarmed and wearing a cloak lined with green, caused considerable comment, bearing in mind his reputation as an able man and his past fortune, for he appeared overcome as if he already knew of his forthcoming death. It is said that when he left his men to come to Senigallia and meet the Duke, he acted as if it were his final parting from them, and that he recommended his household and its future care to his captains and advised his nephews to look to the well-being virtù] of their father's and uncle's households rather than the maintenance of their own. When these three had arrived before the Duke, therefore, and greeted him cordially, they were received by him with a pleasant countenance and it was immediately ensured that they were placed between those who had been designated to take care of them. But when the Duke noticed that Liverotto was not there (for he had stayed with his troops in Senigallia and was waiting in front of the square where his lodgings were, above the river, in order to marshal and drill them), the Duke signalled to Don Michele, who was responsible for taking care of Liverotto, indicating that he should take steps to ensure that Liverotto did not take flight. So Don Michele rode ahead and being met by Liverotto, told him that now was not the time to keep his men in formation outside their quarters because the Duke's men would be taking them over, and therefore he suggested he send his men to their quarters and came with him to meet the Duke. After Liverotto had carried out the order, the Duke arrived and seeing Liverotto, greeted him. Once Liverotto had paid his respects he joined the others. When they had entered Senigallia and all dismounted at the Duke's lodging and entered a secret room with him, they were taken prisoner. The Duke immediately mounted his horse and ordered that Liverotto's and the Orsini's men be robbed. Liverotto's men were all pillaged as they were close by, but the Orsini and Vitelli troops, being at some distance and having anticipated their masters' downfall, had time to fall into formation, and once they had recalled to mind the strength [virtù] and discipline of the Vitelli dynasty, they closed ranks tightly and saved themselves, despite the hostility of the surrounding countryside and the enemy troops. The Duke's soldiers, however, not being content with robbing Liverotto's men, began to sack Senigallia, and if it had not been for the Duke's suppression of their insolence, with the death of many, they would have sacked the whole town.

When night fell and the disturbances had ceased, the Duke decided to have Vitellozzo and Liverotto killed and, leading them to a place together, he had them strangled. At that time, neither of them used words worthy of their former lives, as Vitellozzo begged that he should be able to petition the Pope for a full indulgence for his sins and Liverotto, crying, put the whole blame on Vitellozzo for the injuries suffered by the Duke. Paulo and the Duke of Gravina Orsini were kept alive, but only until the Duke learned that the Pope had seized Cardinal Orsini, the Archbishop of Florence, and messer Jacopo da Santa Croce at Rome.[7] After receiving this news, on 18 January, they too were strangled in the same way at Castel della Pieve.

[7] Rinaldo Orsini was Archbishop of Florence at the time.

THE PRINCE
(De principatibus)

Letter of dedication

Niccolò Machiavelli to His Magnificence Lorenzo de' Medici[1]

Those men who are anxious to ingratiate themselves with a prince are normally in the habit of greeting him either with those things they consider of the greatest value from amongst their own possessions or with objects they perceive give him most pleasure. For this reason one often sees princes presented with horses, weapons, gold-embroidered fabrics, precious stones and similar ornaments commensurate with their grandeur. Being eager, therefore, to offer my services to your Magnificence with some token of my subservience towards you, I have found nothing amongst my most precious and valued possessions of greater worth than my knowledge of the actions of great men, learned through extensive contact with contemporary events and a continual study of the ancients. Now that I have carefully considered and examined these matters at length, I have drawn them together in a small volume which I send to your Magnificence.

Although I do not consider this work worthy to be presented to you, nonetheless I trust that it will be accepted on account of your humanity, bearing in mind that I am incapable of offering you a greater gift than the means to be able to understand in an instant those things that I have learnt and understood through

---

[1] Machiavelli originally intended to dedicate the work to Giuliano de' Medici (1479–1516), but on Giuliano's death he dedicated it to Lorenzo de' Medici (1492–1519), Giuliano's nephew and the grandson of Lorenzo *Il Magnifico* de' Medici (1449–92), who had recently seized control of the duchy of Urbino. He was therefore a new prince taking control of a traditional hereditary principality.

long experience and no little personal hardship and danger. I have not dressed or filled this work with lengthy closures, or magnificent and fine-sounding words, or with any other artifice or superfluous ornamentation, such as many are accustomed to use in describing and adorning their works; for I desired that either nothing at all was worthy in the work, or that the novelty of the treatment and the seriousness of the subject alone rendered it rewarding. Nor, I hope, will it be considered impudent that a man of low and mean station presumes to discuss and arrange the governments of princes. For just as those who draw maps place themselves low down on the plains to consider the nature of the mountains and high places, and place themselves in the mountains and high places to consider the plains, so in the same way it is necessary to be a prince in order to understand clearly the nature of the people and to be of the people to understand the nature of princes. Therefore, your Magnificence, take this small gift in the spirit in which it is offered, and you will find within it, if you read it carefully, my most earnest desire that you attain that greatness ordained by fortune and your own virtues. And, if your Magnificence should periodically cast a downward glance to these lowly parts from the pinnacle of your greatness, you will realise the extent to which, undeservedly, I have to tolerate the great and unceasing malevolence of fortune.

CHAPTER I

The Classification of Principalities and How they are Acquired
(*Quot sint genera principatuum et quibus modis acquirantur*)

All the states and all the governments that have had, and have, power over men have been, and are, either republics or principalities. Principalities are either hereditary, in which case the blood-line of the prince has been long established as ruler, or they are new. These new principalities in turn are either brand new, as was Milan to Francesco Sforza,[2] or they are like limbs joined to the hereditary state of the prince who acquires them, as is the Kingdom of Naples to the King of Spain.[3] The dominions acquired in this way are either used to living under a prince or accustomed to being free; are either acquired with the arms of others or with the prince's own, and either acquired through the agency of fortune [*fortuna*] or on account of personal strength and ability [*virtù*].

CHAPTER 2

On Hereditary Principalities
(*De principatibus hereditariis*)

I will leave aside a consideration of republics as I have already treated the subject at length.[4] My attention will be solely focused on principalities, following the pattern laid out above, and discussing how these principalities can be governed and secured.

I hold, therefore, that with states that are hereditary and accustomed to the blood-line of their prince there is less difficulty in holding on to them than with new ones, since it is sufficient to leave the pre-existing order established by their ancestors undisturbed, and only make alterations as circumstances dictate. In this way a prince who is of average capability will always keep his state unless an extraordinary and excessive force deprives him of it, and should he lose it in this manner he will repossess it at the first setback suffered by the conqueror.

---

[2] Francesco Sforzo (1401–66), the mercenary commander, was hired by Filippo Visconti, Duke of Milan, and married his illegitimate daughter Bianca Maria in 1447. On the Duke's death he served the Milanese Republic defending them from Venetian attack until 1450 when, in a dramatic *volte face*, he sided with the Venetians and entered the city as ruler. See Chapter 7.

[3] Ferdinand II of Aragon, 'the Catholic', seized the Kingdom of Naples from his cousin Frederick I of Aragon through a treacherous alliance signed with King Louis XII of France in November 1500, the secret Treaty of Granada. He subsequently turned on Louis, and made the Kingdom of Naples a Spanish dependency.

[4] According to some critics, Machiavelli is referring to Book I of the *Discourses on the First Ten Books of Titus Livy*, which they claim he began in 1513. However, this assertion is strongly disputed.

In Italy we have the example of the Dukes of Ferrara who paid no attention to the attacks of the Venetians in 1484, nor to those of Pope Julius in 1510, solely on account of the long duration of their rule in that dominion.[5] A natural prince is more loved since he has less reason and less need to offend, and so long as extraordinary vices do not make him hated it is logical that he should be well thought of by his subjects. For the memory of and reasons for innovation are extinguished by the longevity and continuity of rule. Any alteration always leaves the toothing-stone upon which further changes can be built.[6]

CHAPTER 3
On Mixed Principalities
(De principatibus mixtis)

Difficulties are more readily found, however, in newly acquired principalities. Firstly, if the principality is not brand new but like a limb (so the dominion as a whole can be classified as mixed) innovations occur in the first instance as a result of a natural difficulty found in all new principates, namely that men willingly change masters in the hope of improvement. It is this belief that makes them take up arms against the prince. They deceive themselves in this regard, however, as they subsequently discover through experience that their situation has actually worsened. This results from another common and natural necessity which ordains that you must always hurt those responsible for your becoming a new prince, inflicting on them armed soldiers and countless other injuries that follow in the wake of conquest. Consequently all those who have been injured in occupying that principality are enemies, whilst you are unable to keep those who have put you there as friends because of your inability to satisfy them in the manner they had anticipated.

[5] Machiavelli here refers to both Ercole d'Este (1471-1505) and Alfonso d'Este (1476-1534), who held on to their territories despite the continual aggression of both the Venetian and Papal forces.
[6] Toothing-stones are the stones which a builder leaves jutting from a wall to facilitate the addition of further stones by way of extension.

Moreover, given that you are in their debt, you are unable to use strong medicine against them, because you always need the backing of the inhabitants to enter a territory, irrespective of the strength of your army. For these very reasons Louis XII, King of France, occupied Milan straight away and lost it equally quickly, Lodovico's own troops proving sufficient to retake it at the first attempt.[7] This was because those people who had opened the gates for him, finding themselves deceived in their opinion and in the anticipated profit they had taken for granted, were unable to tolerate the vexations of the new prince.

It is a truism that it is only with the greatest difficulty that one loses lands repossessed after a rebellion: for the ruler, seizing the opportunity presented by the rebellion, is less circumspect in securing himself by punishing the malefactors, identifying those under suspicion, and providing for the strengthening of any weaknesses. So, for Milan to be lost to the French on the first occasion, it was sufficient that a Duke Ludovico should make his presence felt at the borders. To lose it the second time required the whole world to be against them and their forces to be destroyed or chased out of Italy.[8] Despite this, Milan was taken from the French on both occasions. The general explanations for the first seizure have already been discussed.

It now remains to examine the reasons for the second loss, and consider what remedies the King of France had at his disposal, and what steps could be taken by someone in similar difficulties to hold on to his conquest more successfully than the King of France did. I propose, therefore, that those states which are joined to the long-established state of a conqueror when they are acquired are either in the same geographical area,

[7] On the death of Gian Galeazzo Sforza, Louis XII sent his forces into Lombardy to lay claim to the duchy of Milan which he occupied briefly before the Milanese drove him out and called Ludovico 'il Moro' Sforza back from the court of the Emperor Maximilian in February 1500, Ludovico himself was subsequently betrayed by the Swiss and died in a French prison in 1512.

[8] Louis XII recaptured Milan from the recently reinstated Ludovico Sforza in April 1500 after the Battle of Novara. He eventually lost control of it again after the Battle of Ravenna in 1512, when he was defeated by the combined forces of the Holy League (Spanish, English and Venetians) under Pope Julius II.

sharing the same language, or they are not. When they are, it is very easy to hold on to them, especially when they are not accustomed to a free way of life. To have them securely in one's grasp, one only has to extinguish the blood-line of the former ruling prince. In all other respects, as long as the former conditions are maintained and there is no alteration to established customs, men live quietly; as illustrated by the cases of Burgundy, Brittany, Gascony and Normandy, which have now been under French rule for so long. And although in this case there are some linguistic differences, nonetheless the way of life is similar and they are able to get along easily together. If the person acquiring such states wants to hold on to them, he should have two concerns: firstly, that the family of the former prince is wiped out, and secondly, that the laws and taxes remain unchanged. In this way, within a very short space of time, the new acquisition will be fused with the old into a single body.

But when states are acquired in an area that has a different language and different customs and institutions, difficulties are inevitable, and you need to be very fortunate and very resourceful to hold on to them. One of the best and most effective cures would be for the conqueror to take up residence there. This would render the possession more secure and more enduring. The Turk did this in Greece.[9] For he would have been unable to hold on to that state, despite all the other precautions taken, if he had not gone to live there himself. If you are there, you can observe disorders arising and apply speedy remedies. If you are not there, however, you become conscious of them only when they have become fatal and all remedies ineffective. Besides, by doing this the area is not plundered by officials and the subjects are satisfied because they have direct access to the prince, and have more reason to love him if they intend to behave well, and fear him if they were thinking of acting otherwise. Anyone from outside who might consider attacking this state should be wary, for the resident ruler can lose it only with the greatest of difficulty.

[9] The Ottoman Turks conquered Constantinople in 1453 after gaining control of most of the Balkan peninsula under successive Sultans.

The other, and better, remedy is to establish colonies in one or two places, which act like fetters in securing that state. It is necessary to do this, the only alternative being to maintain a considerable number of infantry and horsemen there. Colonies do not cost much, and with little or no expense can be established and maintained. The only people harmed are those from whom land and houses are taken to give to new inhabitants and they only constitute a small part of that state. Those who have been injured can never pose any threat as they remain poor and dispersed, and the rest remain on the one hand unoffended (and so should remain quiet) and on the other, have a dread of erring, for fear of the same thing as happened to the dispossessed happening to them. In brief, these colonies cost little, are more faithful, cause less trouble, and, as I said, those who have been offended can do little damage as they are scattered and poor. For it has to be said that men should either be caressed or crushed, for if the injuries are slight they can always gain revenge, but they cannot if they are heavy. So any injury a ruler inflicts on a man must be done in such a way that he need not fear a vendetta. It costs considerably more if you garrison infantry there rather than colonies, because the defence costs will consume all the state's fiscal income, so that on balance the acquisition shows as a loss. In addition, more people are harmed as the army's constant changing of quarters proves injurious to the whole state, and the inconvenience of it is felt by everyone, and they then become the ruler's enemy. Moreover, since they remain defeated in their own homes, they are enemies who are capable of causing you harm. In every respect, therefore, these garrisons are as unprofitable as colonies are profitable.

In addition, a ruler in a province that does not conform with his own as outlined above, should make himself head and defender of the smaller neighbouring powers, whilst seeking to weaken those that are strong. He should also ensure that an outsider with power equal to his own does not enter the province through any unforeseen circumstance. Such an outsider will always be invited in by those who are dissatisfied, either through excessive ambition or fear, as happened before when the Aetolians brought the Romans into Greece.[10] In every other province the Romans invaded they were introduced by the inhabitants. Things develop as follows: as soon as a powerful outsider enters a province all those who are less powerful become his allies, driven by their jealousy of the former ruler. In this way the outsider gains the allegiance of these minor powers with a minimum of effort, for they willingly form a single body with the state he has acquired in that area. He has only to ensure that they do not gain too much strength and authority. He can easily put down those who are strongest with his own forces and the backing of the others, and so remain absolute arbiter of that province. The ruler who fails to manage this aspect of his rule well, will soon lose what he has acquired, and while he holds it, will experience endless internal difficulties and troubles.

The Romans adhered to these policies closely in the provinces they seized. They set up colonies, engaging in friendly relations with the minor powers without increasing their strength, and subdued the powerful. At the same time they did not allow powerful outsiders to acquire any support in the province. The example of the province of Greece is sufficient to prove the point. The Achaeans and Aetolians were appeased by the Romans, the Macedonian kingdom subdued and Antiochus was driven out. The merits of the Achaeans and Aetolians never tempted the Romans into permitting them to extend their states. Neither did the entreaties of Philip induce them into becoming allies before they had diminished his power, nor did the power of Antiochus ever persuade them to consent to his holding any political or territorial power in that province. For in these cases

---

[10] In 211 BC the Aetolians became the first Greek state to ally with the Romans against Macedon. In the passages that follow, Philip of Macedon fulfils the role of ruler, Antiochus III of Syria the powerful outsider and the Aetolians and Achaeans the minor powers. Machiavelli is referring to the sequence of events during the Second Macedonian War (200–189 BC) when the Romans gained control of the territory by defeating the ruler with the help of the minor powers, then allied themselves with the defeated ruler to drive out the external aggressor and finally punished the minor power, the Aetolians, who sought to introduce him. In this way they weakened the various groups and ensured their total dependency on Roman rule.

the Romans did what all wise princes should do: namely, they paid attention not only to current troubles, but also to future ones, seeking to forestall them as diligently as possible. For, in anticipating troubles while they are still hidden it is easy to apply a remedy, but if one waits for the appearance of the symptoms the medicine is too late, as the illness has by then become incurable. In this instance it is true what doctors of consumption say: that in the early stages it is easy to cure but difficult to diagnose, but as time passes, if it has not been identified and treated at the outset it becomes easy to diagnose but difficult to cure. So it is in matters of state: because in recognising early the difficulties that lie hidden in that province (a skill granted only to the prudent) one can rectify them quickly. But when, because they have not been diagnosed, they are left to develop to the extent that everybody can recognise them, there are no longer any effective remedies.

The Romans, however, in identifying hidden problems, always solved them. They never allowed them to continue in order to avoid a war, as they knew that wars never go away but are merely deferred to the advantage of others. For this reason they declared war on Philip and Antiochus in Greece, so as not to have to deal with them in Italy. They could have avoided both of them in the short term, but that was not what they wanted. Nor were they ever tempted to do what we always hear suggested by the so-called wise men of our day: namely to wait and see what tomorrow brings. Instead they enjoyed the fruits of their own strength and skill [virtù] and prudence. For time propels everything forward and can bring with it good as well as bad, and bad as well as good.

But let us return to the example of the King of France and study whether he adhered to any of the provisions mentioned above. I will discuss Louis, and not Charles, because it is easier to chart his progress, as he held on to his possessions in Italy for longer.[11] You will observe how he did the opposite of what one

[11] King Charles VIII was only in Italy between September 1494 and October 1495, whilst Louis XII's forces remained there between 1499 and their defeat at Ravenna in 1512.

ought to do in order to maintain a state in a country which was formed differently from his own.

King Louis was brought into Italy by the ambition of the Venetians who sought to gain half of Lombardy in exchange.[12] I do not want to deride the King's decision, because he was seeking a foothold in Italy without having any allies there (in fact he found all the gates bolted, due to the behaviour of King Charles), and consequently was forced to accept whatever support he could. This wise decision would have turned out well for him had he not made mistakes in other respects. Once the King had acquired Lombardy, therefore, he immediately regained the esteem of which he had been deprived by the actions of Charles. The republic of Genoa ceded, the Florentines became his allies, and the Marquis of Mantua, the Duke of Ferrara, the Bentivogli, the Countess of Forlí, the rulers of Faenza, Pesaro, Rimini, Camerino, Piombino, and the peoples of Lucca, Pisa and Siena all approached him with a view to forming alliances.[13] Only then were the Venetians able to judge the recklessness of the decision they had taken, for in seeking to gain two possessions in Lombardy they made the King of France ruler of a third of Italy.

Consider, on the other hand, with what little difficulty the King could have maintained his esteem in Italy, if he had observed all the rules laid down above and kept his allies under firm control and secure. Because they were numerous, weak, and some fearful of the Church and others of the Venetians, they were constrained by necessity to remain his allies. Through their combined strength he could have secured himself against those who remained strong. But no sooner was he in Milan than he did the opposite by helping Pope Alexander to occupy the

[12] In February 1499 Louis XII made a pact with the Venetians to conquer the duchy of Milan and then cede Cremona and the Ghiara d'Adda to them.
[13] Giovan Francesco Gonzaga was Marquis of Mantua, Ercole d'Este the Duke of Ferrara, the Bentivogli from Bologna, Caterina Sforza Riario Countess of Forlí and Imola, Astorre Manfredi from Faenza, Giovanni Sforza from Pesaro, Pandolfo Malatesta from Rimini, Giulio Cesare da Varano from Camerino and Iacopo d'Appiano from Piombino.

Romagna.[14] Nor did he realise that with this decision he was weakening himself, as he deprived himself both of friends and of those who had thrown themselves on his mercy, whilst at the same time empowering the Church by adding temporal power to the spiritual authority which already gave it such strength. Once the first error had been committed, others were bound to follow. For in order to put an end to Alexander's ambitions and prevent him becoming ruler of Tuscany, Louis was forced to descend into Italy.[15] As if increasing the Church's power and depriving himself of allies was not enough, he then divided Italy with the King of Spain because of his desire for the Kingdom of Naples. Whereas initially he was arbiter of all Italy, he now introduced an accomplice to whom the ambitious people of that country and those discontented with his rule could turn. For whilst he could have left a tributary King to rule Naples, Louis removed him, to replace him with someone with the potential to drive out Louis himself in turn.

The desire to acquire more is very natural and very widespread. When able men fulfil this desire, they will always be praised rather than censured. But when they lack the ability to do so, but still insist at all costs, this constitutes an error and deserves censure. If the King of France, therefore, was able to occupy the Kingdom of Naples with his own forces, he should have done so; if not, he should not have shared it. And if the partition of Lombardy with the Venetians can be excused on the grounds that it enabled him to gain a foothold in Italy, the partition of the Kingdom of Naples deserves censure, as there was in this instance no similar justification.

[14] The Pope was keen to support the ambition of his son Cesare Borgia in the Romagna, and gained the King's approval as the price for annulling his marriage and allowing him to marry Charles VIII's widow, Anne of Brittany. See Chapter 7.

[15] Borgia's success was sufficient to alarm Louis, who descended into Italy after news of the rebellion of Arezzo and the Valdichiana in the summer of 1502. See the beginning of *Duke Vaentino's treacherous betrayal* ... and Machiavelli's other brief tract, *How to Deal with the People of the Valdichiana who have Rebelled*, both of which relate to this period and Machiavelli's involvement in these events.

Louis, therefore, made the following five mistakes: he destroyed the minor powers, increased the strength of a pre-existing power in Italy, introduced a very powerful outsider into that country, did not take up residence there himself, and failed to establish colonies there. These errors alone would not have caused him any harm, had he lived, but he committed a sixth: he seized power from the Venetians. If he had not increased the power of the Church and brought the Spanish into Italy, it would have been more than reasonable, indeed necessary, to weaken the Venetians' power. Once he had decided to follow the first two courses of action, however, he should never have agreed to the Venetians' ruin; because they would have held back the others' designs on Lombardy for as long as they remained powerful. Firstly because the Venetians would never have allowed anyone but themselves to become rulers of Lombardy, and secondly because the others would not have wanted to seize it from France in order to give it to the Venetians. If anyone should say that King Louis ceded the Romagna to Alexander and the Kingdom of Naples to Spain in order to avoid a war, I would reply with the arguments laid out above. Namely, that one should never allow a problem to continue in order to avoid a war because one never avoids it but merely postpones it to one's disadvantage. If others should cite the King's promise to carry out this task in exchange for the settlement of his divorce and the granting of a cardinal's hat to the Archbishop of Rouen, a promise that placed him in the Pope's debt, my reply will be found in the forthcoming section concerning the fidelity of princes and whether they should keep their promises.

King Louis lost Lombardy, therefore, because he failed to follow any of those procedures followed by others who have conquered provinces and wanted to keep hold of them. There is nothing surprising about this, indeed it is easily explained and happens very frequently. I discussed this issue with the Cardinal of Rouen at Nantes, when Valentino (as Cesare Borgia, son of Pope Alexander, was popularly known) was occupying the

Romagna.[16] As a result of the cardinal saying to me that the Italians did not understand warfare, I told him that the French did not understand statecraft. For if the French did understand it, they would never have let the Church acquire so much power. Events have proved that the power of the Church and Spain in Italy was caused by the King of France, and that they subsequently brought about his ruin. From this fact one can deduce a general rule which never, or only rarely, fails. Whoever causes another to become powerful ruins himself, since that power is created by him either through cunning or through force, and he who has become powerful is wary of both of these qualities.

CHAPTER 4

Why the Kingdom of Darius, Conquered by Alexander, did not Rebel against his Successors after Alexander's Death
(*Cur Darii regnum quod Alexander occupaverat a successoribus suis post Alexandri mortem non defecit*)

Considering the difficulties involved in holding on to a newly acquired state, it is easy to wonder how it came about that when Alexander the Great, who became ruler of Asia in the space of just a few years, died after barely establishing himself there, his death did not result in widespread rebellion – an expectation that seems perfectly reasonable. Despite his death, his successors held on to Asia and experienced no difficulties in keeping it, apart from those which emerged between them as a result of their ambition.[17] My answer to this problem is that all the

[16] In October and November of 1500, Machiavelli was at the French court in Nantes on diplomatic business. The Cardinal of Rouen was Georges d'Amboise (1460–1510), chief adviser to Louis XII, and from 1500 lieutenant-general of French forces in Italy.
[17] Alexander the Great (356–23 BC) conquered Asia and the kingdom of Darius III in seven years. After his death four years later, the seven Greek provincial generals who succeeded him fought for control of the empire which resulted in its division into eleven smaller kingdoms, including Macedon, Syria and Egypt.

principalities mentioned in past texts are found to be governed in one of two ways: either by a single prince upon whom all the others are dependent and who, like ministers, help to govern that kingdom with his permission and favour alone, or by a prince together with nobles, who hold their position through their ancient lineage and not through the grace of the ruler. Such nobles have their own states and subjects, subjects who recognise them as their masters and are naturally loyal to them. Those states that are governed by a prince and his officials are held more securely by the prince, because he is without equal throughout his lands. If the people obey anybody else, it is solely as a minister or official, and not due to any affection they feel for the individual concerned.

Contemporary examples of these two types of government are provided by the Turk and the King of France. The whole kingdom of Turkey is governed by one ruler, the rest are his dependants. He divides his kingdom into sandjaks and sends various administrators to them, and changes and moves them around as he sees fit. The King of France, on the other hand, finds himself amongst a crowd of hereditary nobles who are recognised and loved by their subjects. They have their privileges, and the King would deprive them of these only at his peril. Whoever considers these two states, therefore, will find the Turkish state difficult to acquire, but once vanquished, very easy to hold on to. On the other hand, the state of France is more easily conquered in certain respects, but held on to with much greater difficulty.

The reasons why it is difficult to occupy the Turkish Kingdom are, firstly that there is no chance of being invited in by the princes of that kingdom, and secondly that there is no hope of a rebellion by those who surround the ruler to facilitate such an undertaking. This is on account of the reasons mentioned above, for since they are all dependents and bound by obligation to their master, it is more difficult to corrupt them. There is little profit to be gained by successful corruption, as dependants are unable to bring the people with them, for the reasons cited. So, whoever attacks the Turk must bear in mind that he will find them all united. It is probably better for such a person to trust more in his own forces than in the internal divisions of others. But once such a kingdom is conquered and its forces routed in battle, it is incapable of reforming, and the only remaining concern is the prince's blood-line. Once this has been wiped out, no one who is to be feared remains, as the others have no standing in the public eye. And just as the victor, before victory, could not hope for any help from dependants, so afterwards he should not fear any harm from them.

The opposite happens in kingdoms governed like France, because it is easy for you to enter such places if you win over a baron to your cause, for you will always find malcontents and those who desire change. These people, for the reasons already stated, can provide a way into that state and facilitate your victory. Such a victory subsequently trails countless difficulties in its wake, both from those who have helped you and those you have injured, if you wish to hold on to your acquisition. Nor is it enough to wipe out the prince's line, because those nobles are still there and capable of leading further uprisings. Since it is impossible to content the nobles or wipe them out, you lose that state whenever the opportunity presents itself.[18]

Now if you care to consider the type of government Darius ruled, you will find it resembles the Turkish kingdom. And although it was necessary for Alexander to smash everything and seize control of the countryside, after that victory, when Darius was dead, the state remained stable for the reasons discussed above. If his successors had been united they could have enjoyed it at their leisure, as the only tumults that arose in that kingdom were those they brought upon themselves. It is impossible, however, to rule with such serenity states constituted like France. This explains the regular uprisings against the Romans by the Spanish, French and Greeks, which are accounted for by the numerous principalities that existed within

---

[18] Machiavelli's observations on the constitutional structure of France were the result of four diplomatic missions there between 1500–12, and resulted in a separate tract entitled A Portrait of the State of France (c. 1510).

these states. The Romans were never secure in their occupation of these states so long as the memory of these principalities endured. But once this collective memory had been erased by the power and longevity of Roman domination, they established themselves firmly as rulers. When the Romans subsequently began to fight amongst themselves, particular individuals were able to command support from sections of those territories in proportion to the authority that they gained within them. The inhabitants of these territories pledged sole allegiance to the Romans because the line of their former rulers had been wiped out. Bearing in mind all these facts, therefore, the ease with which Alexander the Great held Asia will come as no great surprise. Nor should one be shocked by the difficulties that others experienced in keeping hold of what they had acquired, as the example of Pyrrhus and many others show.[19] The difficulties arose less from any personal shortfall in ability [virtù] on the part of the victor, but rather as a result of the differences in the make-up of the subject territories.

CHAPTER 5

How Cities and Principalities, which Prior
to Occupation were Accustomed to Living under
their Own Laws, Should be Administered
(*Quomodo administrandae sunt civitates vel principatus,
qui antequam occuparentur suis legibus vivebant*)

There are three ways of holding on to those states that one acquires which are used to living freely and under their own laws. The first way is to destroy them. The second is to go and live there oneself. The third way is to let them continue living under their own laws whilst levying a tribute and ensuring they remain your allies by creating well-disposed ruling élites. Given that the state was created by the prince, any élite will know that its standing is dependent upon his friendship and power, and

---

[19] Pyrrhus (319–272 BC) experienced great difficulty in maintaining his conquests in both Greece and Italy.

consequently it will do anything to keep him as ruler. Should you want to keep a city, it is far easier to hold it with the aid of its citizens than in any other way, especially when it is accustomed to living freely.

The Spartans and Romans provide fitting examples. Although they eventually lost them, the Spartans held Athens and Thebes through creating oligarchies. The Romans, in order to hold Capua, Carthage and Numantia, destroyed them and did not lose them. The Romans wanted to rule Greece in the same way as the Spartans had done, allowing the Greeks their liberty and maintaining their laws, but they did not succeed.[20] As a result, they were compelled to destroy many cities in that province in order to keep control of it. For, if the truth be told, there is no better way of possessing them securely than by destroying them. Whoever becomes master of a city accustomed to the free way of life invites his own destruction unless he destroys it first, because in times of rebellion it always has recourse to the name of liberty and its ancient institutions, which, despite the passage of time and the granting of favours, are never forgotten. Anything you implement or plan is useless if you do not set the citizens against each other and scatter them throughout the land, because otherwise they will forget neither the name of liberty nor those institutions, and will turn to them immediately at the slightest chance. This is what Pisa did after a hundred years of Florentine subjection.[21] But when cities and provinces are used to living under a prince they can never agree on a replacement once his blood-line is wiped out. This is because they have no

[20] After conquering Athens in the Peloponnesian War, the Spartans established the rule of the 'Thirty Tyrants' in 404 BC, but were driven out by Trasibulus the following year. The Romans destroyed the towns listed in 211 BC, 146 BC and 133 BC respectively. The Roman conquest of Greece was in two stages, firstly in 196 BC, with the Battle of Cynoscephalae, and secondly in 146 BC, when Corinth was destroyed and Greece made a Roman province.

[21] Florence purchased Pisa from the Visconti of Milan in 1405 and lost it in 1494 when Charles VIII descended into Italy. Its assumption back into the Florentine territorial state was completed in 1509. Machiavelli was extensively involved in the diplomatic and military attempts to retake Pisa in this period, and as Secretary to the Second Chancery and the Ten of War, wrote one of his first formal pieces, entitled *Report on the Pisan War* (1500).

experience of the free life, for they are accustomed to obedience and have lost the old prince. As a result they are slower to take up arms and a prince can more easily gain the state and secure their allegiance to him. But there is more life, more hate in republics, and they have a greater desire for vendetta, and the memory of their ancient liberties never leaves them or allows them to sit back. For this reason the most certain path to take is either to destroy them or to live there yourself.

CHAPTER 6
On New Principalities Acquired by One's Own Forces and Personal Ability
(*De principatibus novis qui armis propriis et* virtute *acquiruntur*)

Nobody should be surprised if I cite the greatest of examples in the following discussion of those principalities that are totally new, by which I mean that they have both a new prince and a new form of government. For, given that men almost always follow the paths set down by others and proceed in their actions by imitation, a prudent man should always follow in the footsteps of great men. He should imitate those who have been outstanding despite the fact that he will be unable to follow their paths exactly or aspire to their personal ability [*virtù*]. Even if his own personal ability [*virtù*] fails to match theirs, at least it will benefit through comparison. He should follow the example of the prudent archers who, when the target they want to hit seems too far away, bear in mind their bows' capability [*virtù*] and set their aim considerably higher than the intended target, with the intention, not of shooting above it, but of reaching it with the help of the high trajectory.

I maintain, therefore, that with principalities that are wholly new and have a new prince the relative difficulty experienced in achieving permanent rule is directly proportional to the personal ability of the prince who acquires it. And since the very act of a private individual becoming a prince presupposes either personal ability [*virtù*] or good fortune, it seems logical that one or other of these qualities should alleviate, in part, many difficulties. Having said that, the prince who owes less to fortune lasts longer. Things are made easier when the prince, not having any other states, is forced to go and live there himself. But to move on to those who became princes as a result of their own ability [*virtù*] and not through fortune, I say that the most outstanding are Moses, Cyrus, Romulus, Theseus and their like.[22] And although Moses ought not to be discussed, on the grounds that he merely carried out what he was told to do by God, the fact that he was considered important enough for God to talk to him should alone render him worthy of our admiration. But let us consider Cyrus and the others who acquired and established kingdoms. You will find them all worthy of imitation. If you consider their actions and the provisions they made as individuals, you will not find them that different from those of Moses, who, after all, had such a great teacher. You can see by examining their actions and their lives that the only thing they got from fortune was the opportunity. This gave them matter which they were then able to form as they saw fit. Without that opportunity the strength and dynamism [*virtù*] of their character would have been stifled, and without that strength and dynamism [*virtù*] the opportunity would have passed in vain.

In this way, for the people of Israel to be prepared to follow Moses in order to escape servitude, it was essential that he found them in Egypt, enslaved and oppressed by the Egyptians. It is just as well that Romulus did not remain on Alba and that he was exposed to die at birth, otherwise he would never have become King of Rome and founder of that land. It was fundamental that Cyrus should find the Persians discontented with the rule of the Medes, and the Medes weak and effeminate because of the long period of peace. Theseus would have been

---

[22] Cyrus the Great ruled the Achaemenid Persian Empire between c. 559–29 BC. Romulus was the mythical founder of Rome discussed by Livy, and Theseus the legendary hero who fought with and killed the Minotaur in the labyrinth. Machiavelli's attitude towards Moses is heavily ironic, in line with his treatment of ecclesiastical principalities in Chapter 11.

unable to demonstrate his strength and dynamism [*virtù*] if he had not found the Athenians dispersed. For this reason, these opportunities made these men happy, and their outstanding strength and dynamism [*virtù*] enabled them to recognise the opportunity when it arrived. As a result of their personal ability, their countries grew in stature and prospered greatly.

Those who become princes through their own ability, as they did, have difficulty in acquiring principalities, but hold on to them with ease. The difficulties that they do have in acquiring a principality are partly caused by the new institutions and procedures that they are forced to introduce in order to lay the foundations of their state and ensure their own security. One should bear in mind that there is nothing as difficult to handle, more dubious in outcome, or more dangerous to organise, than the assumption of responsibility for the introduction of a new form of government. For the person who introduces this new form makes enemies of all those who benefited under the old form, and receives only lukewarm support from all those who would benefit under the new. This half-hearted support is partly due to their fear of their opponents, who have the laws on their side, and partly to the incredulous nature of men. Men do not believe in new things wholeheartedly until they see them firmly established through use. Consequently, whenever enemies of the prince have the chance to attack him, they do it with the strength of a unified faction, whilst the others defend half-heartedly. As a result the new prince is endangered together with them.

In order to consider this argument fully, however, it is necessary to examine whether these innovators are operating on their own account or if they are dependent upon others, that is, whether they rely on requests to do their business or whether they can force the issue. The first way always ends badly and the innovators never achieve anything, but when they rely solely on themselves and can force matters, they are endangered only rarely. This is why all armed prophets are victorious and the unarmed destroyed. In addition to what has already been said, the people are by nature fickle. It is easy to persuade them of something, but difficult to secure them in that conviction. For this reason it is worthwhile being organised in such a way that, when people no longer believe, they can be made to believe by force. Moses, Cyrus, Theseus and Romulus would not have been able to make the people observe their governmental forms for long if they had not been armed. This is what happened in our own time to Fra Girolamo Savonarola, who was destroyed, together with his new institutions, when the multitude began to lose faith in him, for he had no way of holding on to those who had once believed, or of making the disbelievers believers.[23] Innovators who are fortunate at the outset have great difficulty in achieving their ends, for all their dangers arise subsequently as they proceed, and must be overcome by their personal ability virtù]. Once they have overcome these dangers, however, and destroyed those who were envious of their ability, they begin to be esteemed and remain powerful, secure, honoured and happy.

I want to add one minor example to these more lofty ones which will fit well with them and serve to represent all similar examples. I refer to Hieron of Syracuse who, from private citizen, became prince of Syracuse.[24] He also owed fortune nothing but the opportunity. For since the Syracusans were oppressed, they elected him their leader, and he subsequently earned the right to be made their prince. He showed such personal ability [virtù], even in governing the variations of fortune as a private citizen, that his biographer wrote, 'to reign he lacked nothing but a kingdom'. He abolished the old army and organised a new one, dispensed with old alliances and sought new allies, and, given that he had his own allies and

[23] Girolamo Savonarola (1452–98) was the Dominican prior of San Marco in Florence and an evangelical preacher. On the exile of the Medici from Florence in 1494 he assumed political pre-eminence. Unpopular with the Pope for his attacks on the Church's corruption, he was eventually excommunicated and subsequently hanged and burned in the Piazza della Signoria in Florence in May 1498.
[24] Hieron II of Syracuse (c. 308–216 BC). After the departure of Pyrrhus from Sicily, he led the Syracusans against the mercenary soldiers who were occupying Messina. Machiavelli's account of his exploits and tactics is drawn from Polybius's History, I, 8–16, the quotation from Justinian, XXIII, 4, 15.

soldiers, was able to build whatever structure he wanted on
those foundations. Although it took him considerable effort to
acquire that state, it required much less to keep it.

CHAPTER 7
On New Principalities Acquired with the
Forces and Fortune of Others
*(De principatibus novis qui alienis armis
et fortuna acquiruntur)*

Those private citizens whom fortune alone makes princes,
become so with little effort but remain so only with the greatest
of effort. They encounter no difficulties on their ascent – as they
shoot to the top. All their difficulties begin once they have
arrived. This applies to those who receive a state either in
exchange for money, or through the favour of the person who
concedes it. This happened to many in Greece whom Darius
made rulers of the cities of Ionia and Hellespont, so that they
could hold those cities for his glory and security. The same
happened to those emperors who as private citizens came to rule
the empire through the corruption of the soldiers. These people
depend simply on the goodwill and fortune of those who gave
them the state, and goodwill and fortune are very changeable
and unstable things. They do not know how to hold, nor are
they capable of holding, such a position. They do not know,
because, unless they are men of great natural talent and ability
[*virtù*], it is not reasonable to expect them to know how to
command, having only had to deal with fluctuations in personal
fortune. They are incapable, because they do not have their own
well-disposed and faithful military forces. But then again, states
which come on quickly, like all other things in nature that take
seed and grow too fast, cannot form their roots and branches.
Consequently they perish in the first bad weather. This will
happen to men like this who have suddenly become princes and
are, as I have said, of insufficient ability [*virtù*]. They cannot
prepare themselves in an instant to keep what fortune has

thrown into their laps, nor can they construct those foundations that most have built before becoming princes.

I want to cite a couple of examples which have happened within living memory: Francesco Sforza and Cesare Borgia. They exemplify the two ways of becoming a prince as already mentioned – through personal ability [virtù] or by fortune. Francesco became Duke of Milan having previously been a private citizen by using the appropriate means and his own great ability [virtù], and what he acquired with countless anxieties, he kept with little effort.[25] Cesare Borgia, on the other hand, popularly known as Duke Valentino, acquired his state through the good fortune of his father and lost it when his father's fortunes changed.[26] This happened despite his employing every means and doing all the things a prudent and able man should do to establish his roots in those territories which had been given him by the arms and fortune of others. If in the first instance the foundations are forgotten, it requires great ability [virtù] to lay them later, as has already been stated. Moreover, it is inconvenient for the builder and endangers the building. If one considers the Duke's actions, it will be seen that he established strong foundations for future power. I do not consider it superfluous to discuss these foundations, as I know of no better precepts to give to a new prince than the example of the Duke's actions. If he failed to profit from the provisions he made, it was not his fault, but the responsibility of the extraordinary and excessive malignity of fortune.

When Alexander VI sought to make his son, the Duke, powerful, he faced considerable difficulties, both present and future. Firstly, he did not see any way of making his son a ruler of a territory that did not belong to the Church. He knew that once he began to prepare to seize one from the Church, the Duke of Milan and the Venetians would prevent him, because Faenza and Rimini were already under the protection of the

[25] Francesco Sforza (1401–66), see note 2 above.
[26] Cesare Borgia (1475–1507), son of Pope Alexander VI and also known after 1498 as Duke Valentino. From 1499 Cesare commanded the Papal forces in central Italy.

Venetians. He also saw that the armies in Italy, and especially those he could have usefully deployed, were in the hands of those who had reason to fear the growth of the Pope's power. Consequently, he was unable to rely on them, as they were all followers, or members, of the Colonna and Orsini factions.[27] It was therefore necessary for him to disturb those governments and disarrange their states in order to be able to make himself secure ruler of part of them. This was easy for him, as he found that the Venetians, for different reasons, wanted to bring the French back into Italy. Not only was Alexander in favour of this, he made it easier by annulling King Louis' first marriage. The King of France descended into Italy, therefore, with the help of the Venetians and the blessing of Alexander. No sooner was the King in Milan than the Pope received troops from him for the campaign in the Romagna, and the Romagna was handed to him on account of the King's reputation.

Once the Duke had acquired the Romagna and defeated the Colonna, two things prevented him from retaining it and pushing further ahead. First, the fact that he doubted the loyalty of his forces, and second, the desires of the French. For the Orsini troops he had used might leave him stranded, and not only prevent him from acquiring more, but also seize what he had already taken. He also feared that the King might do the same. He had confirmation of these fears about the Orsini forces when, after he had taken Faenza by storm, he assaulted Bologna and saw them go into battle half-heartedly. As for the King, his intentions became clear when the Duke attacked Tuscany after having taken Urbino and was forced by the King to halt the

[27] The Colonna and Orsini were the two major Roman noble families, both famous as mercenary leaders and rivals in the Papal Court. They were led by Cardinal Giovanni Colonna and Cardinal Giovan Battista Orsini respectively. The Colonna were initially supportive of Alexander VI against his uncle, Pope Calixtus III, but later sought his replacement. The Orsini, however, initially his enemies, became his allies. With the election of Julius II della Rovere as Pope in 1503, however, the Colonna's fortunes improved, the Orsini's having declined somewhat earlier, due to their opposition to Cesare Borgia's expansionism. The Cardinal was assassinated in February 1503, and Signor Paulo Orsini and the Duke Gravina Orsini strangled by Borgia at Senigallia.

campaign. As a result, the Duke decided not to depend on the forces and fortune of others any longer. First of all, he weakened the Orsini and Colonna factions in Rome through winning over all their followers who were landed nobles. He secured them by granting them commissions, government posts and honours in keeping with their rank. In this way, within a few months, the attachment they felt for their factions was forgotten and wholly transferred to the Duke. After this, he waited for the opportunity to destroy the leaders of the Orsini to present itself, having already scattered the leaders of the Colonna family. A good chance came his way, and he exploited it to the full. For once the Orsini realised, belatedly, that the increasing power of the Duke and the Church was their undoing, they called a diet at Magione near Perugia. This gave rise to the rebellion of Urbino, the uprisings in the Romagna and endless threats to the Duke, all of which he overcame with the help of the French. Once he had regained his standing, he trusted neither the French nor any other outside forces, and in order not to have to run the risk of trusting them, he turned to deceit.[28] He was so good at disguising his true intentions that even the Orsini, through Signor Paulo, were reconciled with him. For the Duke used every means at his disposal to bind Paulo to him, giving him money, clothes and horses, so much so that the simplicity of the Orsini led them to Senigallia and into his hands. With the leaders dead and their followers secured as his friends, the Duke had laid fairly strong foundations for his power. He controlled all the Romagna and the duchy of Urbino, and, most of all, he considered he had acquired the friendship of the Romagna and won its people over to his cause, as they were beginning to enjoy the taste of prosperity.

I do not want to leave this subject just yet, as it merits closer examination and deserves to be imitated by others. When the Duke seized the Romagna, he found it ruled by weak lords who were more likely to rob their subjects than correct them, giving

[28] Cesare's deceit is fully chronicled by Machiavelli in his piece *Duke Valentino's Treacherous Betrayal* . . ., see pp.28–35.

the subjects reasons for discord rather than concord. Consequently, the province was overwhelmed by thefts, disputes and
every other kind of insolent behaviour. The Duke judged it
necessary to institute good government in order to restore the
state to peace and render it obedient to kingly rule. He therefore
sent messer Remirro de Orco there, a cruel and expedient man,
to whom he granted full powers. Within a short time Remirro
pacified and united the province, and won great acclaim. The
Duke then decided that such excessive authority was not needed,
since he feared that it might become hated, and he established a
civil tribunal there, in the middle of the province, which was
overseen by a well-known senior judge and made up of the legal
representatives sent by each of the towns. And since he knew
that his previous harsh provisions had earned him a degree of
hatred, and wanting to purge that hatred from the minds of the
people and win them over wholeheartedly to his cause, he
sought to demonstrate that if any cruelty had occurred it did not
originate from him, but from the harsh character of his minister.
Taking the opportunity to rectify this, one morning at Cesena
the Duke had Remirro decapitated and his body placed in the
main piazza with a block and bloodied knife by his side. The
savage nature of this spectacle satisfied and intimidated the
people at the same time.

But let us pick up where we left off. I was saying that the
Duke still had to consider the King of France in his desire to
continue acquiring territory, even though he found himself
relatively powerful and partially secured against present dangers. He was armed as he wished and had destroyed the majority
of those forces nearby which were capable of injuring him. He
knew that he would not be supported by the King, who had
only recently realised his error. Consequently, he began to seek
new friends and vacillate in relation to the French during their
progress towards the Kingdom of Naples to fight the Spanish
who were besieging Gaeta. His intention was to secure himself
against the French, an intention he would soon have realised if
Alexander had lived.

These were his actions in relation to current matters. With

regard to the future, he had to consider the possibility that the new successor to the Papacy might not prove friendly and might seek to take from him what Alexander had granted. He thought of four ways of securing himself should this happen. Firstly, he wiped out all the descendants of the rulers he had deposed to deny the Pope the opportunity of using them against him. Secondly, as noted above, he sought to win over all the landed nobles in Rome in order to use them to restrain the Pope, and thirdly, he sought to control, as much as possible, the College of Cardinals. Finally, he sought to acquire enough power before the Pope's death to enable him to resist an initial onslaught unaided. On the Pope's death, he had carried out three of these four aims, and the fourth was almost completed. He murdered as many of the deposed rulers as he could lay his hands on, only a few surviving. He had won over the Roman landed nobles and had the majority of the College of Cardinals on his side. As for the acquisition of new territory, he had planned on becoming the ruler of Tuscany,and already held Perugia and Piombino, Pisa being under his protection. He could have swooped on Pisa as he no longer had to consider the King of France (he did not have to do this any more, as the French had already lost the Kingdom of Naples to the Spanish, so that both sides needed to purchase his friendship). After this, Lucca and Siena would have ceded at once, partly to spite the Florentines and partly through fear, and the Florentines would have been unable to stop them. If he had managed to do all these things (which he would have done in the same year that Alexander died) he would have acquired such strength and standing that he would have been able to stand alone, and not depend any longer on the forces and fortune of others, but entirely on his own strength and personal ability [virtù]. Alexander, however, died within five years of Valentino beginning to wield his sword. He left the Duke mortally in and only the government of the Romagna consolidated, and all the others in mid-air, caught between two extremely powerful enemy armies. The Duke was a man of such ferocity and personal ability [virtù], and the foundations that he had laid in such a short time were so well grounded, that if he had not been up against those armies, and if he had been in good health, he would have withstood every difficulty. He understood so clearly that men must be either won over or destroyed. That his foundations were strong is obvious: although he was barely alive the Romagna waited for him for more than a month; in Rome he was safe from attack; the Baglioni, Vitelli and Orsini were unable to raise a following against him despite the fact that they came to Rome, and though he could not dictate who became Pope, he could dictate who did not. If he had been healthy at the time of Alexander's death, everything would have been easy for him. He told me on the day that Julius II was elected Pope that he had thought of what might happen on the death of his father and had made suitable provision for all eventualities, except for the one possibility that at the time of his father's death he too would be at death's door. This had never occurred to him.

Having considered all the Duke's actions, therefore, I find it difficult to criticise him. If anything, it seems to me that he is worthy to be held up as a model, as I have done, to all those who have risen to power either with the arms of others or through fortune. For he was a man incapable of governing in any other way, due to his great spirit and his tendency to aim high. The only things that stood in the way of his plans were the brevity of Alexander's life and his own illness. Whoever judges it necessary to do the following things in his own new principality cannot find more recent examples to follow than the Duke's actions: to secure himself against his enemies; to win friends; to conquer (whether by force or fraud); to make himself loved and feared by the people and followed and respected by his soldiers; to destroy those who can or might injure him; to alter the established orders by creating new ones; to be severe and well-liked, magnanimous and generous; to destroy disloyal militias and create new ones; and to maintain the friendship of kings and princes in such a way that they must either act beneficently towards you in a gracious manner or take care in injuring you. The Duke can only really be criticised for the election of Julius II as Pope, in that he chose badly. For, as has been said, although he was unable to create a Pope of his liking, he could have prevented the election of somebody he opposed. He should never have allowed the Papacy to go to one of those Cardinals he had offended, nor to somebody who, once elected, had cause to fear him, for men attack either through fear or hate. The following were some of the people the Duke had injured: the Cardinals of San Pietro ad Vincula, Colonna, San Giorgio and Asciano. All the rest had reason to fear him in the event of their being elected Pope, with the exception of the Cardinal of Rouen and the Spanish cardinals, the latter due to their bonds of kinship and the obligations resultant from their favoured status, the former on account of his strength which was derived from the support of the Kingdom of France. For this reason the Duke's first priority should have been to make a Spaniard Pope, and, if this were not possible, to ensure it went to the Cardinal of Rouen and not San Pietro ad Vincula. Whoever believes that ancient wrongs are forgotten by great people in the receipt of new favours is deceived. The Duke, therefore, was mistaken in this election, and it proved to be the cause of his final downfall.

CHAPTER 8

On Those who Acquire Principalities through Wicked Deeds
(*De his qui per scelera ad principatum pervenere*)

Since there remain two further ways in which a private citizen can become a prince, neither of which are wholly attributable to fortune or personal ability, it seems worth including them, even though one of them can be considered at greater length where republics are discussed. They are, respectively, when a person arrives at a principality by a wicked and nefarious route, and when a private citizen becomes leader of his country with the backing of his fellow citizens. In considering the first way, I shall use two examples, one ancient and one modern, without other-

wise entering into the merits of the issue, since I judge it
sufficient that the person who needs to, simply imitates them.

Agathocles the Sicilian became King of Syracuse despite
having been not only a private citizen but also of the most
humble and abject birth.[29] At every stage this man, the son of a
potter, unerringly maintained a wicked life. Nevertheless, his
wickedness was allied with such strength [virtù] of body and
spirit that, having joined the militia, he rose through its ranks to
become praetor of Syracuse. When he was appointed to that
post he decided to become prince and keep by force, and without
regard to his obligations to others, what had been conceded to
him by common consent. Having entered into secret negotiations concerning his plan with Hamilcar the Carthaginian,
who was campaigning in Sicily with his forces, he called together
the people and Senate of Syracuse one morning as if he had
matters to discuss relating to the republic. At a prearranged
signal, he had his soldiers kill all the senators and the richest
members of the people. With their death, he occupied and held
the rulership of that city without any civic upheaval. And
although he was defeated and besieged twice by the Carthaginians, not only was he able to defend his city, but, leaving a
section of his forces to resist the siege, he attacked Africa with
the rest, and within a short time lifted the siege of Syracuse and
drove the Carthaginians to dire straits, so that they were
constrained to make an accord with him in which they had to
settle for possession of Africa and leave Sicily to Agathocles.

Whoever studies the actions and life of this man, therefore,
will notice little or nothing that can be attributed to fortune,
since, as noted above, he came to be prince without the help of
anyone else and by rising through the ranks of the militia whose
support he won by overcoming a thousand difficulties and
dangers. He subsequently maintained his position by adopting
many courageous and dangerous policies. Yet the meaning of
the term virtù does not extend to killing one's fellow citizens,

[29] Agathocles (361–289 BC), the legendary ruler of Syracuse. Machiavelli
derives his story from Justinian XXII.

betraying one's friends, breaking one's word and being merciless and irreligious. These methods can help to acquire power, but not glory. For if one considers the strength and personal ability [*virtù*] of Agathocles in tackling and withstanding difficulties, and the extent of his courage in tolerating and overcoming adversities, it is unclear why he should be judged inferior to any other highly esteemed commander. Nevertheless, his ferocious cruelty and inhumanity and countless iniquities do not allow him to be eulogised as one of the most distinguished of men. One cannot, therefore, attribute to either fortune or *virtù* what was achieved without the aid of either.

In our own times, during the Papacy of Alexander VI, Oliverotto da Fermo, who some years previously had been left fatherless at an early age and raised by a maternal uncle called Giovanni Fogliani, was sent as a youngster to serve as a soldier under Paulo Vitelli, so that versed in that art he might achieve an important military position.[30] With the death of Paulo he served under the latter's brother, Vitellozzo, and in a very short time he became the chief commander of his forces on account of his ingenuity and physical and mental courage. But since he considered it servile to remain on the same footing as others, he planned to occupy Fermo with the support of Vitellozzo and the help of several citizens of Fermo for whom servitude was more dear than the liberty of their land. So he wrote to Giovanni Fogliani explaining how, since he had been away from home for several years, he wanted to return to visit Giovanni and his city, and reacquaint himself in some way with his patrimony. He added that since he had striven for nothing else besides the acquisition of honour, he wanted to make a triumphal entry accompanied by a hundred of his friends and dependants on horseback in order to show his citizens that he had not spent his time in vain. He also begged him to be so kind as to ensure that

---

[30] Oliverotto da Fermo (c. 1475–1502) was another mercenary commander who learnt his trade with the Vitelli and subsequently served under Cesare Borgia. He seized command of Fermo in 1502, in a manner clearly reminiscent of Agathocles. He was killed by Borgia in 1502. See *Duke Valentino's Treacherous Betrayal*, pp. 28–35.

he was received honourably by the people of Fermo, for this would not only bring honour to himself, but also to Giovanni, as Oliverotto was his protégé. Giovanni did not fail in any duty owed to his nephew, and having organised his honourable reception by the people of Fermo, he housed him in his own residence. After several days there, and having secretly seen to the arrangements necessary for his forthcoming wicked act, he organised a stately banquet to which he invited Giovanni Fogliani and all the leading men of Fermo. And when they had partaken of the various dishes and all the other entertainments usually provided at such banquets, Oliverotto artfully broached certain important issues, discussing the power of Pope Alexander and his son Cesare, and their various ventures. Whilst Giovanni and the others were discussing these issues he suddenly stood up saying that these were matters to be debated in a more private place, and withdrew to a room, with Giovanni and all the other citizens following in his wake. No sooner were they sat down than soldiers appeared from secret hiding places in the room and murdered Giovanni and all the others. After this massacre, Oliverotto immediately mounted his horse and rode through the town and besieged the supreme council in the Palace so that they were compelled to obey him through fear and establish a government of which he made himself prince. With the death of all those who would have been discontented with his rule and capable of injuring him, he strengthened his position with new civil and military institutions, so that within a year of holding the principality he was not only secure within Fermo itself, but also feared by all the town's neighbours. His expulsion would have been as difficult as that of Agathocles, had he not allowed himself to be tricked by Cesare Borgia when, as mentioned above, Borgia seized the Orsini and Vitelli at Senigallia. For Oliverotto was also taken and, a year after murdering his adopted father, strangled together with Vitellozzo, the man who had nurtured his personal abilities [virtù] and wickedness.

Some people may wonder how it could come about that Agathocles and those like him, after endless betrayals and cruelties, were able to live securely in their lands for such a long

time, defending themselves from external enemies and un-
troubled by citizen conspiracies against them, whilst many
others, despite their cruelty, have not been able to keep hold of
their rule in times of peace let alone in the uncertain times of
war. I think this depends upon whether cruelty is well used or
badly used. Those forms of cruelty that are deployed in one fell
swoop on account of the necessity of securing oneself are well
used (if one is permitted to speak well of ill) as long as they are
not continued further but rather turned as much as possible to
the advantage of the subjects. The forms of cruelty that are
badly used are those which although initially few and far
between become more frequent with the passage of time rather
than disappearing. Those who follow the first method have some
means of redeeming themselves with God and mankind for their
actions, as did Agathocles. It is impossible for the others to
maintain their hold on power.

Therefore, it is worth noting that in seizing a state the occupier
should consider all the injuries that he must necessarily commit,
and then commit them all at once, so that he does not have to
repeat them every day. For then, by not renewing them, he is
able to reassure men and win them over by granting them
favours. Whoever does otherwise, either through timidity or
through following bad advice, is always compelled to keep a
knife in hand. Nor can he ever place too much reliance upon his
subjects, or his subjects feel secure with him, because of the
current and recurring injuries. For since injuries are less palata-
ble, they should be inflicted all at once so they cause less offence,
while favours should be granted little by little so that they are
more appetising. Above all, a prince should live with his subjects
in such a way that no unforeseen circumstance, be it good or
bad, compels him to alter his conduct. When, in times of
adversity, necessity dictates, evil deeds are already too late, and
good deeds of no use as they judged forced, and not worthy of
thanks.

CHAPTER 9
On Civil Principalities
(*De principatu civili*)

Let us now turn to the second way, namely when a private citizen becomes prince of his land with the support of his fellow citizens rather than through wickedness or intolerable violence. I maintain that one accedes to a principality of this kind (which can be called a civil principality and is normally acquired by fortunate cunning rather than personal ability [*virtù*] or fortune alone) either through the support of the people or the nobles. For one finds these two different humours in every city, and these contrasting humours result in the nobles desiring to control and oppress the people whilst the people desire not to be controlled or oppressed by the nobles. These two differing appetites give rise to one of three possible outcomes: a principate, a state of freedom, or a state of licence.

The principality is either created by the people or the nobles, depending on which of these factions gets the opportunity. For once the nobles perceive they cannot resist the people, they begin to augment the standing of one of their number and then make him prince in order to enable them to satisfy their appetite. Equally, when the people perceive they cannot resist the nobles, they increase the standing of one of their number and make him prince so that they can be defended by his authority. He who becomes prince with the aid of the nobles finds it more difficult to stay in power than he who becomes prince with the aid of the people, for he finds himself surrounded by many who consider themselves his equal, and consequently is unable to govern and manage them as he would wish. The person who becomes prince with the support of the people, however, finds himself alone, with nobody, or very few, who are not prepared to obey him. Moreover, one cannot honestly satisfy the nobles, as is easily done with the people, without injuring others. For the people's aim is more honest than that of the nobles, as the latter seek to oppress while the former seek to avoid oppression. In addition, a prince can never secure himself against a contrary populace on account of their number. He can secure himself against the nobles, however, as they are few in number. The worst a prince can expect from a contrary people is to be abandoned by them. With the nobles as enemies, however, he must not only fear being abandoned, but also that they might move against him. Since they are more perceptive and cunning, they always look ahead to safeguard themselves and seek to ingratiate themselves with whoever they think might win. Necessity also dictates that a prince must always live with the same people, whereas he can get by well enough without the same nobles. Each day he can create and destroy them, depriving or augmenting their standing at will.

In order to make this argument a little clearer, I maintain that nobles should be seen as conforming to two main types, either managing their affairs so that they bind themselves wholly to your fortune, or not. Those who bind themselves to you should be honoured and loved, so long as they are not rapacious. Those who do not commit themselves can be judged in two ways: they act either out of weakness or a natural lack of spirit. In this instance you should make use of them, especially those who can give good advice, because in times of prosperity they will honour you, and you will have no cause to fear them in times of adversity. But when they deliberately fait to commit themselves through ambition, it shows that they are more self-interested than concerned about you. The prince should guard himself against these nobles, and fear them as he would declared enemies, for they will always help to ruin him in times of adversity.

A person who becomes prince with the support of the people, therefore, should seek to retain their friendship. This is easy for him, as they only ask him not to oppress them. But someone who becomes prince with the backing of the nobles, and against the people's wish, must, first and foremost, seek to win over the people. This is also easy for him to do when they seek his protection. And since men bind themselves more tightly to their benefactor when they receive something good having expected something bad, so the people become more well disposed

towards their benefactor than if he had been carried to power
with their backing. There are many ways in which the prince
can win them over, ways which vary according to circumstance
and cannot therefore be drawn together under a general rule. As
a result I will leave them aside. The only conclusion I will make
is that it is necessary for a prince to possess the friendship of the
people, otherwise he will have no remedy in times of adversity.

Nabis, the Spartan prince, withstood being besieged by the
whole of Greece and a victorious Roman army, and defended
his country and his position as prince against them.[31] Once the
danger had arrived, all he had to do was secure himself against
a few subjects. If the people had been his enemy, this would not
have sufficed. Let nobody try to counter this opinion of mine
with that trite proverb which states that he who builds on the
people builds on mud. That may well be true when a private
citizen lays his foundations there, and then assumes that the
people will rescue him should he be threatened by enemies or
magistrates (in which case he could often find himself deceived,
as did the Gracchi in Rome and messer Giorgio Scali in
Florence).[32] But if the prince who lays his foundations on the
people knows how to command, if he has heart and does not
despair in adversity, if he is careful in preparing for other
eventualities and encourages everyone with his spirit and policies, he will never find himself deceived by the people and it will
become apparent that he has built his foundations well.

These principalities are usually endangered when the transi-
tion from civil to absolute government is made. For these princes
rule either on their own account or through magistrates. In the
latter case their position is weaker and more dangerous, as they
are wholly dependent on those citizens who are eligible for

---

[31] Nabis the Spartan (c. 240–192 BC) ruled the city from 207 BC onwards,
and was forced to surrender Argos to combined Roman and Greek forces in
195 BC, although he managed to hold on to Sparta.

[32] Tiberius and Gaius Gracchi (c. 163–21 BC) were tribunes of the plebes and
responsible for the introduction of agrarian reforms which, according to
Machiavelli in the Discourses, were responsible for the fall of Rome. Giorgio
Scali (c. 1350–82) led the revolt of the Ciompi wool workers in Florence in
1378, but was killed in 1382.

public office. These people can easily deprive princes of their position, either through moving against them or refusing to obey them. When the prince is in danger, it is too late for him to seize absolute power because the citizens and subjects, accustomed to receiving orders from the magistrates, will not take them from him in times of crisis. He will also find it difficult to find people he can trust in times of uncertainty. For a prince of this kind cannot rely upon what he observes during peaceful times when the citizens need the state, because at that time everybody runs, everybody promises, and everybody wants to die for him, so long as death remains at a distance. But when the state needs its citizens during times of adversity there are then precious few to be found. This experience is all the more dangerous in that it can only be undergone once. For this reason a wise prince must think of a means whereby his citizens are always in need of the state and of him, whatever the nature of the times. Only then will they always be faithful to him.

CHAPTER 10

How the Strength of Every Principality Should be Measured
(Quomodo omnium principatuum vires perpendi debeant)

It is worth bearing another consideration in mind when examining the nature of these principalities, namely whether, if needs be, a prince has sufficient power to be able to stand alone, or whether he always needs to be protected by others. In order to make this argument a little clearer, I say that princes who can rule by themselves are those who, in my view, are capable of putting together an army which can do battle with any attacking force, either with money or through access to the necessary manpower. Likewise, I consider those who are unable to face the enemy in open battle, but are compelled to take refuge inside the walls and defend them, as always having need of others. The first case has already been discussed and will, in future, be treated as it arises. In the second case one can say little, beyond encouraging such princes to fortify and supply their own cities and pay no attention to the surrounding countryside. People will be very circumspect in attacking a prince who fortifies his city well and manages his affairs with his subjects in the manner laid out above and mentioned below. For men are always hostile to enterprises when they foresee difficulties, and attacking a prince who has a well-defended city and well-disposed populace is not an easy undertaking.

The cities of Germany are totally free, have little surrounding territory and obey the Emperor only when they want to. They do not fear him or any other neighbouring power, as they are fortified in such a way that everybody is aware that it would be a tedious and difficult exercise to vanquish them. For they all have well-placed walls and moats, all the artillery they need and enough food, drink, and fuel for a year housed in their public stores. In addition, they keep enough supplies under public control to be able to furnish the people with the means to ply their trades for a whole year without loss to the public purse. These are the life and soul of the city, and the means whereby the people earn a living. They also consider military exercises important, and as a result have many provisions and institutions relating to their upkeep.[33]

A prince who has a strong city, therefore, and does not make himself hated cannot be attacked, and even if someone did attack him, the aggressor would have to retreat in shame. For worldly matters are so variable, that it is almost impossible that someone could remain encamped with their army for a whole year doing little else. If anyone should object, saying that the people would lose patience if they saw their possessions beyond the city burnt, and that the long siege and self-interest would make them forget their prince, my answer would be that a powerful and spirited prince will always overcome these difficulties, filling his subjects with hope that the ills are nearly

[33] This section summarises some of the observations made by Machiavelli in his A Portrait of German Affairs (1508), see pp. 20–7.

ended, reminding them of the cruelty of the enemy and securing himself speedily against those who appear too outspoken. Besides, the enemy can reasonably be expected to burn and lay waste the surrounding countryside on his arrival at a time when men's spirits are still fired up and dedicated to defence. The prince, therefore, has even less reason to worry, for by the time spirits have cooled after a few days, the damage is already done, the ills inflicted, and there is no longer any remedy. The people will then be even more united with their prince, for they will consider him in their debt, as their houses were burnt and their lands destroyed in his defence, for it is in men's nature to consider themselves bound equally by the favours they confer as by those they receive. So, if all this is borne in mind, it is not difficult for a prudent prince to keep up the spirits of his subjects during a siege, so long as there is enough to live on and the means to defend oneself.

CHAPTER 11
On Ecclesiastical Principalities
(De principatibus ecclesiasticis)

Now it only remains for us to discuss ecclesiastical principalities, which present difficulties prior to being possessed. For they are acquired either through personal ability or fortune and held on to without the help of either, because they are sustained by the ancient rules and institutions of the Church which have been of such strength and of such a type that they keep their princes in power irrespective of how they act and live. These princes alone have states and do not defend them, subjects and do not govern them. As the states are not defended they are not seized from them, and as the subjects are not governed they are unconcerned and do not think, nor are they capable, of changing their princes. These principalities alone, therefore, are secure and content. But I will leave aside a discussion of these principalities since they are governed by higher powers, powers whose reasoning lies beyond the comprehension of the mortal mind. As these

principalities are exalted and maintained by God, only a presumptuous and rash man would assume to discuss them. Nevertheless, someone might well ask me how it came about that the
Church achieved such great temporal power, given that before
Alexander VI was Pope the Italian potentates (and not only
those who called themselves by that name but every baron and
lord, even of the slightest importance) paid it little heed. For the
Church now makes the King of France tremble and was able to
drive him out of Italy and ruin the Venetians. My answer would
be that although the matter is well known it would still be worth
examining again in some detail.

Before Charles, King of France, passed into Italy, that country
was ruled over by the Pope, the Venetians, the King of Naples,
the Duke of Milan and the Florentines. These potentates had to
be wary of two things in particular: firstly, that no outsider
should enter Italy with armed forces, and secondly, that none of
them should attain any more power. They had to be particularly
wary of the Pope and the Venetians. As happened in the defence
of Ferrara, a union of all the others was necessary to hold the
Venetians in check, and in Rome the barons successfully kept
the Pope subdued.[34] Since the barons were divided into two
factions, the Orsini and Colonna, there was always cause for
scandal between them and they were constantly at daggers
drawn under the Pope's very eyes, keeping the Papacy weak and
impotent. And although a courageous Pope, like Sixtus IV,
would periodically emerge, neither fortune nor wisdom would
allow him to overcome this obstacle.[35] This was due to the
brevity of their lives, because in the ten years that a Pope on

---

[34] The war between Venice and Ferrara broke out in 1482, when Ferrara
sought to establish its independence. They were joined in an alliance against the
Venetians by the Papacy, Alfonso, King of Naples, the Florentines and Ludovico
Sforza. The peace of Bagnolo of 1484 confirmed their liberation from Venetian
rule.

[35] Pope Sixtus IV della Rovere (1414–84) was not only a learned man who
enhanced the reputation of Roman papal humanism by expanding the Vatican
library and building the Sistine Chapel, but he also sought greater power for the
Papacy within the Italian peninsula, which involved him in wars with Florence
in 1478–9, and Venice in 1482–4.

average lived, there was barely time to bring down one of the factions. If, for example, one Pope had almost wiped out the Colonna faction, another would arise who was an enemy of the Orsini, and would revive the Colonna without there being sufficient time to destroy the Orsini.

This resulted in the temporal power of the Pope being little respected in Italy. Alexander VI later rose to the Papacy, and he, of all the Popes that have ever lived, demonstrated how much a Pope could achieve with money and armed forces. Through the agency of Duke Valentino and the opportunity afforded by the French descent into Italy he achieved all those things I discussed above concerning the Duke's activities. And although his intention was not so much to increase the Church's power as the Duke's, what he did nevertheless increased the power of the Church, as it inherited the fruits of his labour after he died and the Duke was killed. Pope Julius succeeded him and found the Church powerful, as it possessed all the Romagna, the Roman barons crushed and the factions destroyed by the persecutions of Alexander. He also discovered a ready means of accumulating money which had never been used by Alexander or any of his predecessors. Julius not only inherited this state of affairs, but also sought to improve upon it, planning to take Bologna, destroy the Venetians and drive the French out of Italy. He managed to achieve all these tasks, deserving even more praise as he did it all to increase the Church's power and not that of any individual.[36] He also kept the Orsini and Colonna factions in the state he found them, and although some of their leaders were for revolt, two things kept them in check. Firstly, the power of the Church which frightened them and secondly, they did not have any cardinals who were traditionally the source of all troubles between them. These factions will never be peaceful so long as they have cardinals, because cardinals cultivate the factions both within Rome and beyond, and the barons are forced to defend them. The conflicts and uprisings between the

[36] Pope Julius II entered Bologna on 11 November 1506, driving out Giovanni Bentivogli as part of his campaign to regain control of the Papal States.

barons, therefore, arise from the ambition of the prelates. His Holiness Pope Leo, therefore, found the Papacy very powerful, and it is hoped that what others made great with arms can become even greater and revered on account of his goodness and countless other qualities [virtù].

CHAPTER 12

On the Different Types of Army and the Question of Mercenary Troops
(Quot sint genera militiae et de mercenariis militibus)

Now that I have discussed in detail the characteristics of those principalities that I set out to consider at the start, and having considered to some extent the reasons for their well being and their ill health and shown the means employed by many to acquire and keep hold of them, it now remains for me to discuss in a general manner the offensive and defensive strategies that can occur in each of the forms mentioned above. We have already said how it is necessary for a Prince to have strong foundations, otherwise he will, by necessity, be ruined. The main foundations of every state, whether they be new or old or mixed, are sound laws and sound arms. And since sound laws cannot exist where there are no sound arms, and where sound arms exist it is fitting to have sound laws, I will leave aside a discussion of laws and speak of arms.

I propose, therefore, that the arms with which a prince defends his state are either his own, mercenary, auxiliary or a mixture of the three. Mercenary and auxiliary forces are useless and dangerous, and anyone whose state is based on mercenary arms will never be either well established or safe, for mercenaries are disunited, ambitious, lacking in discipline and untrustworthy. They are brave in the company of friends and cowardly in the face of the enemy, they are neither God-fearing nor loyal to their fellow men, and they prevent ruin only so long as they are not challenged. In times of peace you will be robbed by them, in times of war by the enemy. The reason for this lies in the fact that there is no desire or reason to remain in the field besides a measly stipend, which is hardly sufficient to induce them to die on your behalf. They are well disposed to be your soldiers so long as you do not declare war, but with the coming of battle they either take flight or desert. It should not be difficult for me to persuade you of the truth of this matter, since the ruin of Italy has been caused by nothing other than its reliance on mercenary arms for so many years. And although they made some advances for some people and appeared brave when fighting against each other, when the foreigner arrived they showed their true colours. Consequently, Charles, King of France, was allowed to seize Italy with a piece of chalk. The person who said that the cause of this was our own sins spoke the truth, although they were not the sins that he thought but the ones I have just outlined.[37] And since they were the sins of princes, princes have also paid the price for them.

I want to illustrate more clearly the failure of these troops. Mercenary leaders are either excellently versed in arms or they are not. If they are, you cannot trust them as they will always aspire to personal greatness either by oppressing you as their patron or through oppressing others without your permission. If the leader is not personally capable he will usually ruin you anyway. Should someone reply that whoever has arms at hand would do likewise, whether or not he be a mercenary, I would answer that arms should be wielded either by a prince or a republic. The prince should go in person and do the leader's job himself. The republic should send its citizens, and when it sends one who does not turn out to be a brave man, it should change him, and if he is, it should bind him with laws to ensure he does not overstep the mark. Experience shows that only princes and armed republics make great progress, whilst mercenaries achieve nothing but harm. A republic with its own forces is less easily

[37] This is a satirical jibe at Savonarola, 'the unarmed prophet', and his Florentine sermon of 1 November 1494, when he blamed Florentine difficulties on the sins of its citizens. At the time Charles VIII and his forces were threatening Florence.

subjected by one of its own citizens than a republic armed by foreign troops.

Rome and Sparta remained armed and free for many centuries. The Swiss are very strongly armed and enjoy complete freedom. The Carthaginians provide an ancient example of mercenary forces. They were nearly subjugated by their mercenary soldiers after the first war with the Romans, despite the fact that they were led by their own citizens. After the death of Epaminondas, the Thebans made Philip of Macedon captain of their forces. After victory, he deprived them of their liberty. Similarly, after the death of Duke Filippo [Visconti], the Milanese hired Francesco Sforza to fight the Venetians. Once he had defeated the enemy at Caravaggio he joined with them to oppress the Milanese, his patrons. His father, Sforza, having been hired by the Queen of Naples, suddenly left her defenceless, thereby forcing her, for fear of losing her kingdom, to throw herself on the mercy of the King of Aragon. That the Venetians and Florentines have, in the past, increased their power with these troops, and that their commanders have defended them rather than become their princes, is due to good luck in the Florentines' case. For of the capable commanders they might have feared, some failed to win, some were opposed and others directed their ambition elsewhere. John Hawkwood was the one who failed to win, and in not winning it is impossible to gauge his fidelity, although everybody agrees that if he had won, the Florentines would have been at his mercy.[38] Sforza always had the Bracceschi against him, so that they were always wary of each other. Francesco directed his ambitions towards Lombardy, and Braccio against the Church and the Kingdom of Naples.[39]

[38] Sir John Hawkwood (c. 1320–94), known as Giovanni Acuto, was an English mercenary leader who fought extensively in Italy, working almost exclusively for the Florentines from 1380 onwards. He was considered an outstanding commander, but all his military undertakings were defensive. He was commemorated in the Cathedral of Florence with a fresco portrait by Paolo Uccello in 1436.

[39] The 'Bracceschi' were the armed followers of Braccio da Montone (1368–1424) who were defeated by Francesco Sforza (1369–1424) at the Battle of Aquila. Earlier, in 1416, Braccio had gained control over Umbria. Francesco

But let us turn to what happened recently. The Florentines made Paulo Vitelli, a most prudent man, their commander, and from humble beginnings he gained considerable standing. Nobody denies that if he had taken Pisa by storm the Florentines would have been compelled to stay with him, because had he been hired by their enemy they would have had nowhere to turn. If they were to keep him, they would have to obey him. If you consider the policies followed by the Venetians you will notice that they functioned securely and gloriously whilst they fought with their own arms (namely prior to turning their attentions to campaigning on the mainland), the patricians and armed militia performing outstandingly well. But when they began to fight on the mainland, they abandoned this good practice [virtù] and adopted traditional Italian military habits. At the beginning of their territorial expansion they had little to fear from their commanders as their state was small and their standing great. They first tasted the error of their ways during their territorial expansion under Carmagnola. For while they noted Carmagnola's exceptional ability when they conquered the Duke of Milan under his leadership, they also noted his lack of enthusiasm for the war and judged that further victories under his leadership were unlikely, as he had lost the desire to fight. However, they could not afford to release him for fear of relinquishing what they had already acquired. So they were constrained by necessity to kill him in order to secure themselves against him.[40] They then had Bartolomeo da Bergamo, Roberto da San Severino, the Count of Pitigliano and their like as their commanders – men who caused the Venetians to fear the loss of what they already had, rather than hope for any gain, as subsequently happened at Valià where they lost in a

Sforza, like Hawkwood, was employed several times as a mercenary by the Florentines. 'Sforza' here refers to Francesco's father, Munzio Sforza (1369–1424).

[40] Francesco Bussone da Carmagnola (1390–1432) was a mercenary commander who served under the Visconti of Milan against Venice, although he subsequently changed masters, fighting for the Venetians against the Visconti and winning the Battle of Maclodio in October 1427. The Venetians had him killed in May 1432.

single day's battle what they had acquired over eight hundred years with considerable effort.⁴¹ These troops only give rise to slow, tardy and weak acquisitions and sudden and incredible defeats. And since these examples have brought me to Italy, which has been ruled by mercenary armies for many years, I want to discuss mercenaries at greater length so that, having observed their origin and development, they can be used more profitably.

You must realise, therefore, that as soon as Italy began to strike back against the Empire, and the Pope began gaining more standing in the temporal sphere, Italy was divided into more states. Many of the larger cities raised arms against their nobles who had previously held them in subjection with the backing of the Emperor, while the Church supported them in order to increase its temporal standing. In many other cases the citizens became princes. As a result, when Italy was almost wholly in the hands of the Church and a few republics, and as those priests and citizens were unversed in military matters, they began to hire foreign mercenaries. The first to gain credibility for this kind of army was Alberigo da Conio, from the Romagna.⁴² Braccio and Sforza were both products of Conio's military training and arbiters of Italy in their prime. After them came all the rest who, up until now, have managed armies like these. The result of their collective talents [virtù] has seen Italy conquered by Charles, looted by Louis, seized forcibly by Ferdinand and shamed by the Swiss. The policy they instituted was first of all to belittle the worth of the infantry in order to

⁴¹ Bartolomeo Corleone da Bergama (1400–75), an outstanding military leader of his day, served nearly all the major Italian powers before leading the Venetian forces from 1454. He was defeated by Francesco Sforza at the Battle of Caravaggio in 1448. Roberto da San Severino (1418–87) fought under the Sforzas before assuming command of the Venetian forces in 1482 against Ferrara. Niccolò Orsini (1442–1510), the Count of Pitigliano, served the Venetians between 1495 and 1510, and was the leader of their forces in the fateful Battle of Vailà in 1509.

⁴² Alberigo da Conio (1348–1409) was a mercenary commander who fought with Hawkwood in the Romagna and formed an Italian mercenary force known as the company of Saint George. He also served with the Visconti, the Papacy and the King of Naples.

increase the standing of their own forces. They did this because the small numbers of infantry did not give them any standing, and, lacking states and working as mercenaries for a living, they were unable to support large numbers of them. So they concentrated on cavalry, which were more easily provided for if in manageable numbers, and brought them some honour. Matters came to such a pass that in an army of twenty thousand there were less than two thousand infantry. Moreover, they used every means possible to relieve themselves and their soldiers of any exertion or fear, by not killing each other in combat but rather taking each other prisoner without ransom. They did not move against cities at night, and those in the cities did not attack the camps. They never built stockades or ditches around their camps and they did not camp out during the winter. All these things were sanctioned by their military codes, and cited by them in order to avoid both exertion and danger, as has been said. Consequently, they have reduced Italy to slavery and shame.

CHAPTER 13

On Auxiliary Troops, your own Troops, and a Mixture of the Two
(De militibus auxiliariis, mixtis et propriis)

Auxiliary troops, which are the second kind of useless soldier, are those sent when you ask a powerful ruler to help to defend you with his troops. Pope Julius did this recently when, having observed his mercenary force's poor performance during the Ferrara campaign, he turned to auxiliaries and arranged for the soldiers and armies of Ferdinand, King of Spain, to help him. These troops can be useful and effective in their own right. However, they are almost always harmful to those who have recourse to them, as if they lose, you are undone; if they win, you become their prisoner. And despite the fact that ancient history is full of such examples, I nevertheless want to stay with the recent example of Pope Julius II, whose policy could not have been more ill conceived, for in seeking to gain Ferrara, he threw himself wholly into the hands of a foreigner.[43] His good fortune, however, gave rise to a third factor which prevented his reaping the harvest of his bad choice, for when his allies were routed at Ravenna, and when the Swiss arose and drove off the victors, contrary to his own and everybody else's expectations he found he was neither the prisoner of his own armies who had fled, nor of his auxiliaries, as the battle had been won by others' arms and not theirs. The Florentines, being totally without military provisions, brought ten thousand French troops to Pisa to take it by storm, a policy which put them in greater danger than at any other time during their difficulties. The Emperor of Constantinople sent ten thousand Turks into Greece to oppose his neighbours, but when the war was over they refused to leave, marking the beginning of the subjection of Greece by the infidel.[44]

A prince who does not want to win, therefore, should use auxiliary troops, for they are far more dangerous than mercenaries. Ruin is inevitable because they are totally united and completely set in obeying others. Mercenaries, however, need more time and a greater pretext to attack you once they have won, as they are not a unified body and have been sought out and paid by you. If you appoint a third party to lead them, he cannot instantly assume sufficient authority to be able to harm you. In short, with mercenaries indolence is more of a danger, whilst with allies the danger is their collective strength [virtù].

Wise princes, therefore, have always avoided auxiliary troops and depended on their own, preferring to lose with their own than win with another's, not judging what is acquired with alien forces a true victory. I will never hesitate to cite the example of

[43] See note 34 above.
[44] The Emperor of Constantinople referred to by Machiavelli was John Cantacuzenus (c. 1292–1383). With Turkish help he won the civil war in 1347 after he had seized the crown from the ruling Palaelogus dynasty and declared himself emperor. The Turks then captured Gallipoli from him in 1354, marking the start of their campaign to capture Greece.

Cesare Borgia and his actions. This duke entered the Romagna with auxiliary arms, and deployed a force composed entirely of French troops there, seizing Imola and Forlì with them. But when he subsequently perceived that such forces were unsafe, he turned to mercenaries, judging them less dangerous, hiring the Orsini and Vitelli. When he discovered in dealing with them that they were also unreliable, untrustworthy and dangerous, he destroyed them and turned to his own forces. One can easily see the difference that exists between the two types of arms by considering the increase in the Duke's prestige when he relied upon his own troops and his own strength, compared with previously, when he had only the French, or the Orsini and Vitelli troops. Each time he grew in strength, and at no stage was he more highly rated than when everybody saw that he was in complete command of his own forces.

Although I do not want to depart from examples which are both recent and Italian, I do not want to neglect Hiero of Syracuse, whom I mentioned above. He immediately realised the uselessness of the mercenary army when, as I said, the people of Syracuse made him commander of their forces, for they were hired hands in the same mould as our Italian ones. And when he perceived that he could neither keep them on nor let them go, he had them all cut to pieces, subsequently waging war using his own troops and not those belonging to another. In addition I would like to call to mind an allegory from the Old Testament which illustrates this point. When David offered to go and fight the Philistine challenger Goliath on Saul's behalf, Saul gave David his own arms to give him courage. After David had put them on, he rejected them saying that he was unable to acquit himself well with them, preferring to seek out the enemy with his sling and his knife.

In short, the armour of others either falls off your back, weighs you down or restricts your mobility. Charles VII, father of King Louis XI, recognised the necessity of arming himself with his own forces when he freed France from the English through a combination of good fortune and personal ability [*virtù*].[45] He immediately established provisions to raise cavalry and infantry in his kingdom. King Louis, his son, then dispensed with those governing the infantry and began to hire the Swiss. This error, followed by others, is clearly the reason why that Kingdom now finds itself in such peril. Having placed more value on the Swiss forces, he debased the rest of his army. He abolished the infantry altogether, and made the cavalry dependent upon others' troops, so that they did not consider themselves capable of victory without the Swiss troops with whom they had become accustomed to train. This led to the French being numerically inferior to the Swiss, and not daring to fight anyone else without them. The French armies, therefore, have been mixed, part mercenary and part their own troops, and when joined together they are much better than auxiliaries on their own or just mercenaries, but much inferior to one's own troops. The example cited should prove sufficient, as the Kingdom of France would be unbeatable if the provisions made by Charles had been developed and maintained. But lack of prudence in men means they begin something which, because it tastes good at the start, gives no indication of the poison that lurks beneath the surface, as I mentioned above in relation to consumption.

Therefore, he who fails to recognise evils when they arise in a principality is not truly wise. This gift is granted to few. If one considers the primary cause of the downfall of the Roman Empire it is seen to have begun solely with the hiring of the Goths, since from that beginning the debilitation of the forces of the Roman Empire started and all the strength and ability [*virtù*] taken from the Romans was passed to the Goths.

I conclude, therefore, that no principality is secure without its own army. Indeed, it is wholly dependent upon fortune, having no strength that can be relied upon to defend it in times of adversity. It has always been the opinion and dictum of wise

[45] Charles VII brought the Hundred Years War to an end in 1453, expelling the English from France, with the exception of Calais which they still held. The military provisions referred to by Machiavelli were enforced between 1445–8, and established a permanent national body of cavalry and infantry, the *compagnies d'ordonnance* and the *francs archers*.

men that, 'nothing is weaker or more unstable than a reputation for power which is not based on one's own power'.[46] One's own power at arms is composed of either subjects, citizens or dependants, as all the rest are either mercenaries or auxiliaries. The way to organise one's own troops will be easily revealed if one examines the military provisions taken by the four men I mentioned above, and if one observes the manner in which Philip, the father of Alexander the Great, and many other republics and princes have acted. Personally, I swear by their strictures.

CHAPTER 14
How a Prince Should Act Concerning Military Affairs
(*Quod principem deceat circa militiam*)

A prince, therefore, should have no concern, no thought, or pursue any other art besides the art of war, its organisation and instruction. This is the only art that those who command are expected to master. This art has such potency [*virtù*], that not only does it ensure that those who are born princes remain princes, but it often enables men of humble rank to rise to that position. By contrast, it is noticeable that when princes have paid more attention to luxuries than to arms, they have lost their states. Loss of state results primarily from neglecting this art, whilst being proficient in it will lead to the acquisition of state.

Francesco Sforza, formerly a private citizen, became Duke of Milan because he was armed. His sons, because they avoided the inconvenience of armies, became private citizens having formerly been dukes. For, amongst the other things that will bring difficulties, being unarmed will bring contempt. This is one of the infamies against which a prince must guard, as I will make clear later, as there is no comparison between a man who is armed and a man who is not armed. It is unreasonable to

[46] Tacitus, *Annales*, XIII, 19.

expect that an armed man should willingly obey one who is unarmed, or that an unarmed man should feel secure surrounded by armed subordinates. For when one party is contemptuous and the other suspicious, it is impossible for them to work well together. A prince who fails to understand military matters, therefore, in addition to other difficulties, as stated, can neither be respected by his troops nor place his trust in them.

He should never, therefore, cease to think about the occupation of being a soldier, and should exercise more vigorously in times of peace than in times of war. This he can do in two ways, physically and mentally. As far as physical exercise is concerned, in addition to keeping his army well organised and trained, he should always be out hunting. This will help him both to accustom his body to discomfort and to learn something of the lie of the land, so that he knows where the mountains rise up, where the valleys narrow down and how the plains extend, and observes the characteristics of the rivers and marshes. He should take great care in all this. This knowledge is useful in two ways. Firstly, he becomes familiar with his own country and better understands how to defend it. Secondly, through his knowledge and experience of those areas, he can more easily understand every other area that it might be necessary for him to spy out. For the hills, the valleys, the plains, the rivers and the marshes of Tuscany, for example, have a certain similarity to those of other regions, so that from a knowledge of how the land lies in one region, he can easily come to understand another. The prince who lacks this skill, lacks the first attribute that a commander must possess, since it teaches him how to locate the enemy, where to strike camp, how to lead armies, plan battles and besiege towns to his advantage.

Philopoemen, leader of the Achaean League, was praised by the historians for, amongst other things, not thinking of anything else apart from military strategy during peacetime.[47] Often

---

[47] Philopoemen (253–184 BC) was a mercenary commander who became leader of the Achaean League. See also Chapter 3. Machiavelli's source was Livy, *Ab urbe condita*, XXXV, 28.

when he was in the countryside with his friends he would stop and discuss with them: 'If the enemy were on that hill, which of us would hold the advantage? How could you march to engage with them without breaking ranks? If we wanted to retreat, how should we do it? If they were to retreat, how should we pursue them?' and, as they went along, he put forward to them all the possible scenarios that could confront an army. He would heed their views, and give his own, backing them up with reasons, so that through this continual cogitation nothing could unexpectedly arise while he was leading his armies for which he did not have a remedy.

As regards the training of the mind, the prince should read histories, and observe the actions of outstanding men contained in them, noting how they acted in times of war, examining the reasons for their victories and defeats in order to be able to imitate the former and avoid the latter. Above all, he should do what certain outstanding men did in the past, in taking someone who has been praised and glorified before them as a model for imitation, always keeping their actions and deeds close at hand. It is said that Alexander the Great did this in imitating Achilles; Caesar, Alexander; and Scipio, Cyrus. And whoever reads the life of Cyrus written by Xenophon, will then realise the extent to which that imitation resulted in Scipio's own glory during his lifetime, and how much Scipio's chastity, affability, humanity and liberality conformed with those self-same qualities in Cyrus as described by Xenophon.

A wise prince should follow these kinds of practice, never remaining idle in times of peace but seeking rather to profit from such peace assiduously, in order to be able to make use of it in times of adversity, so that when fortune changes her mind, he finds himself prepared to withstand her.

CHAPTER 15
On the Things for which Men, and especially
Princes, are Praised or Blamed
(*De his rebus quibus homines et praesertim
principes laudantur aut vituperantur*)

It now remains to consider the procedures and policies a prince should adopt in relation to both his subjects and allies. And since I am aware that many have written on this theme, I am afraid that, in also writing about it myself, I may be considered presumptuous, especially as I depart from the methods adopted by others when discussing this subject. But since my intention is to write something useful for the understanding reader, it seems to me more beneficial to go behind to the effectual truth of the matter, rather than focusing on the imagining of it. For many writers have depicted their own republics and principalities which have never been seen or known actually to exist. And since the distance between how one lives and how one should live is so great, he who discards what he does for what he should do, usually learns how to ruin rather than maintain himself. For a man who wants to make a career of doing good in all spheres will be ruined amongst so many who are not good. Therefore, it is necessary for a prince, if he wants to mantain his position, to develop the ability to be not good, and use or not use this ability as necessity dictates.

Leaving aside the imagined aspects of a prince, therefore, and discussing those that are real, I maintain that all men, when they are talked about, and especially princes, since they are more exposed, are remarked upon for various qualities which bring them either praise or blame. For some are considered generous, others miserly (to use a Tuscan term, since avaricious, in our tongue, still refers to someone who desires to possess something by force, whilst we call somebody who refrains from using his own things miserly). Some are considered benefactors, others greedy; some cruel, others merciful; some faithless, others trust-worthy; some effeminate and weak, others fierce and bold; some humane, others proud; some lascivious, others chaste; some upright, others cunning; some severe, others easy-going; some serious, others light-hearted; some religious, others sceptical and so on. I realise that everyone will admit that it would be most laudable to find all the good qualities mentioned above combined in a prince. But since it is not possible either to possess or wholly to observe them, because human nature does not allow it, it is necessary for him to be sufficiently prudent that he knows how to avoid the infamy of those vices that will deprive him of his state, and, if at all possible, be wary of those that are less threatening. If this is impossible, however, he should not worry unduly about the latter. Moreover, he should not worry about the infamy incurred by those vices which are indispensible in maintaining his state, because if he examines everything carefully, he will find that something which seems virtue [*virtù*] can, if put into practice, cause his ruin, while another thing which seems a vice can, when put into practice, result in his security and well-being.

CHAPTER 16
On Generosity and Meanness
(*De liberalitate et parsimonia*)

Let me begin, therefore, with the first of the qualities mentioned above. I maintain that it would be good to be considered generous. Nevertheless, generosity, when used in such a way as to gain you that reputation, will damage you. Because if it is used virtuously and as it should be used, it is not recognised, and you will not avoid the infamy of its opposite. Therefore, if you want to establish a name for yourself as a generous person, you cannot afford to neglect any kind of lavishness. A prince who acts this way will soon use up all his resources and will eventually, if he wishes to maintain a name for being generous, be constrained to impose extra taxes in addition to the normal levies, and be rigorous and do all he can to acquire money This will begin to make him odious to the people, and little esteemed on account of his poverty. Consequently, having harmed the majority and rewarded few with his generosity, he will feel the effect of difficulties immediately and be endangered by the first threats that arise. When he realises this and seeks to exercise restraint, he will instantly acquire the reputation of a miser.

Therefore, as a prince cannot employ and gain a reputation for this virtue [*virtù*] of generosity without damaging his position, he should not mind, if he is a prudent man, being called a miser. With the passage of time he will be considered increasingly generous, and given that his income from taxes will be sufficient for him, due to his parsimony, he will be able to defend himself against those who declare war on him, and to launch campaigns without burdening the people with taxes. Consequently, he displays generosity to all those from whom he takes nothing, who are countless in number, and miserliness to all those to whom he gives nothing, who are few. In our own times we have seen great things achieved only by those who have been held miserly. The others have been wiped out. Pope Julius II, who used his reputation for generosity to accede to the Papacy, did not consider keeping it up later, since he wanted to be capable of fighting wars. The current King of France has waged many wars without levying any additional taxes on his subjects, solely because his enduring parsimony has underwritten the extra expenditure. The current King of Spain would not have launched, or won, so many expeditions if he had been reputed generous.

A prince, therefore, should give little thought to being considered miserly if it means not robbing his subjects, being able to defend himself, not becoming impoverished and contemptible, and not being forced to become rapacious. For this is one of those vices which enables him to rule. If anyone should say, 'Caesar rose to power through generosity, and many others have reached the highest positions because they were considered, and were, generous', I would reply, 'You are either a prince already, or you are in the process of becoming a prince. In the first instance this kind of generosity is harmful, in the second it is necessary to be considered generous. Caesar was one of those who wanted to become ruler of Rome, but if, having arrived at that position, he had survived and not tempered his spending, he would have destroyed that power.' And if anyone should answer, 'There have been many princes who have achieved great things with their armies and been held generous', I would reply, 'The prince either spends what is his own and his subjects', or what belongs to others. In the first instance he should be thrifty, in the second unsparing in his generosity. The prince who accompanies his armies, and who lives off plunder, pillage and ransoms, uses what belongs to others. It is necessary for him to be generous, otherwise he would not be followed by his troops. For he can be a more munificent benefactor when handling what does not belong to himself or his subjects, as Cyrus, Caesar and Alexander were. Because disposing of what belongs to others does not diminish your standing but adds to it. Dispensing with what belongs to yourself is the only thing which will harm you, for there is nothing more self-destructive than generosity, because as you practise it you lose the ability to practise it, and become either impoverished and contemptible or, in order to avoid poverty, rapacious and odious. Being thought contemptible and odious are amongst the things a prince should guard against, and generosity can lead to both the one and the other.' It is wiser, therefore, to be reputed miserly, which breeds infamy but not hatred, than, in seeking to be held generous, being forced to gain a reputation for rapacity, which breeds infamy combined with hate.

CHAPTER 17

On Cruelty and Mercy; and Whether it is Better
to be Loved than Feared, or the Reverse
(*De crudelitate et pietate; et an sit melius
amari quam timeri, vel e contra*)

Passing down the list of the aforementioned qualities, I maintain that each prince should desire to be thought merciful and not cruel. Nonetheless, he should be careful not to misuse this mercy. Cesare Borgia was considered cruel, nevertheless his cruelty put the Romagna in order, uniting it and reducing it to peace and loyalty. If one examines this carefully, you will see that he was far more merciful than the Florentine people, who, rather than be thought cruel, let Pistoia destroy itself.[48] A prince, therefore, should pay no heed to the infamy of being considered cruel if it means he keeps his subjects united and loyal. For he will be more merciful by making an example of one or two people than those who allow disorders to continue, resulting in murders and theft due to misjudged mercy. For these disorders usually harm the whole community, whilst the executions a prince orders harm only a single person. The new prince, above all other princes, cannot avoid a reputation for cruelty, since new states are full of dangers. Virgil says in the following words of Dido,

> difficult circumstances and the newness of my kingdom constrain me to undertake these things, and defend my frontiers everywhere with guards.[49]

Nonetheless, he should be circumspect in believing and acting, and not be afraid of his own shadow, proceeding in a manner tempered by prudence and humanity, so that over-confidence does not make him hasty, or excessive mistrust render him intolerable.

This gives rise to an argument: whether it is better to be loved than feared, or the opposite. The answer is that one would like to be both, but since it is difficult to combine the two it is much safer to be feared than loved, if one of the two has to make way. For generally speaking, one can say the following about men: they are ungrateful, inconstant, feigners and dissimulators, avoiders of dangers, eager for gain, and whilst it profits them

---

[48] Pistoia's long-standing factions, the Cancellieri and the Panciatichi, resumed virtual civil war after the exile of the Medici from Florence in 1494. Machiavelli made at least three visits to the town in an attempt to quell the factions and enforce the *Capitoli*, peace treatises instituted by the Florentine commissioners. In March 1502 he wrote a brief tract entitled *De rebus pistoriensibus*.

[49] Virgil, *Aeneid*, I, 563–4.

they are all yours. They will offer you their blood, their property, their life and their offspring when your need for them is remote, as mentioned above. But when your needs are pressing, they turn away. The prince who depends entirely on their words perishes when he finds he has not taken any other precautions. This is because the friendships that are purchased with money and not by greatness and nobility of spirit are paid for, but not collected, and when you need them they cannot be used. Men are less worried about harming somebody who makes himself loved than someone who makes himself feared, for love is held by a chain of obligation which, since men are bad, is broken at every opportunity for personal gain. Fear, on the other hand, is maintained by a dread of punishment which will never desert you.

Nonetheless, the prince should make himself feared in such a way that, even if he is not loved, he avoids being hated, since being feared and not hated can easily go together. This will always happen if he abstains from the property of his subjects and citizens, and from their womenfolk. If he should need to take anyone's life, he should do it when there is a suitable justification and a demonstrable cause. But above all, he should abstain from other's property, since men forget their father's death more quickly than the loss of their patrimony. Moreover, there is never a shortage of reasons for taking property, and the prince who begins to live by robbery finds reasons to sequester what belongs to others. With executions it is the opposite, reasons are more exceptional and less numerous.

But when the prince is with his armies and in charge of a large number of soldiers, then it is very necessary that he does not worry about a reputation for cruelty. Amongst Hannibal's admirable actions is the following: that having led an incredibly large army, made up of countless different races, on campaigns in foreign lands, no dissension ever arose either among the troops themselves or against their leader, irrespective of whether they enjoyed good or bad fortune. This came about for no other reason than his inhuman cruelty, which, together with his other infinite abilities [virtù], made him respected and feared in the eyes of his soldiers. Without it, and the effect it had, his other abilities [virtù] would not have been enough. The historians, paying scant attention to the matter, on the one hand admire his achievement whilst simultaneously condemning its main cause.

The truth of the assertion that his other abilities [virtù] would not have been enough, is seen in the case of Scipio, a man not only exceptional in his own time but also in the annals of all that is known, for his armies rebelled against him in Spain. This happened solely on account of his excessive mercy, which granted more licence to his soldiers than is fitting for military discipline. He was reproached for this in the Senate by Fabius Maximus, who called him the corrupter of the Roman legions. Scipio failed to ensure that the people of Locri were avenged after they had been plundered by one of his legates, nor was the legate in question punished for his insubordination. All this happened due to his accommodating nature. So much so that when some sought to excuse him before the Senate, they noted that many men knew better how not to err than how to punish those who erred. Scipio's nature would, in time, have ruined his fame and glory if he had continued acting this way during his rule. But when he lived under the rule of the Senate, this harmful quality of his remained not only hidden, but even brought him glory.[50]

Returning, therefore, to the subject of being feared or loved, I conclude that since men are loving when it suits them and fearful when it suits the prince, a wise prince should base himself on what is his, not on what belongs to others. He should merely seek, as I said, to avoid hatred.

[50] Scipio Africanus the elder (c. 236–183 BC) was the leader of the Roman armies in Spain, who drove out the Carthaginians and then launched a campaign in northern Africa, defeating Hannibal and capturing Carthage in 201 BC. The Locri episode is taken from Livy, Ab urbe condita, XXIX, 8–21. See also Chapter 14.

CHAPTER 18
Whether Princes Should Keep Their Word
(*Quomodo fides a principibus sit servanda*)

Everyone understands how laudable it is for a prince to keep his word and live with integrity and not cunning. Nonetheless, experience shows that nowadays those princes who have accomplished great things have had little respect for keeping their word and have known how to confuse men's minds with cunning. In the end they have overcome those who have preferred honesty.

You must understand, therefore, that there are two ways of fighting: the first using laws, the second force. The first belongs to man, the second to animals.[51] But since the first is often not enough, one must have recourse to the second. It is therefore necessary for a prince to know how to make good use of the animal and the human. This precept was taught to princes by the ancients under the cover of allegory. They wrote how Achilles and many more of those ancient princes were entrusted to Chiron the centaur for their upbringing, so that they could be looked after under his tutelage.[52] Having a half-man, half-beast as a teacher simply means that a prince needs to know how to use both natures, for the one without the other does not last.

As it is necessary for a prince to know how to use the animal, therefore, he should choose the fox and the lion from amongst their ranks, since the lion cannot defend itself from traps and the fox cannot defend itself from the wolves. One needs to be a fox, therefore, to recognise traps, and a lion to frighten the wolves. Those who rely simply on the lion do not understand this. A prudent ruler, therefore, cannot, and should not, keep

[51] Machiavelli here touches on a widespread behavioural analogy. This particular passage refers to Cicero, *On Duties*, I, xiii. Other commentators have also pointed to Dante, *The Divine Comedy*, Inferno, XXVII, 74–5. Machiavelli was also aware of the lion and the wolf story in Aesop's *Fables*, 42, as witnessed in Vettori's letter to him of 23 November 1513. See p. 3.

[52] The other rulers referred to are Hercules, Jason, Asclepius and Theseus.

his word when keeping it is to his disadvantage, and when the reasons that made him promise no longer exist. For if all men were good, this precept would not hold good, but since they are bad and would not keep their word to you, you do not have to keep yours to them. Nor is there ever a shortage of legitimate reasons to disguise your disregard. Countless current examples could be cited of this, showing how many peaces, how many promises have been rendered null and void through the untrust-worthiness of princes. The one who has known how best to use the fox has come off best. But it is necessary to know how to disguise this nature well and be a great feigner and dissimulator. Men are so simple and so obedient to present needs, that he who deceives will always find people who will let themselves be deceived.

Of the recent examples, I would like to mention one in particular. Alexander VI never did anything, nor thought of anything, apart from deceiving men, and he always found a subject who would enable him to do it. Never was there a man more effective in swearing, who affirmed things with such heavy oaths, and yet stuck to them less. Nonetheless, his deceptions always worked out as he hoped, because he well understood this aspect of life.

It is unnecessary, therefore, for a prince actually to have all the qualities mentioned above, but it is more than necessary to seem to have them. Indeed, I will hazard to say this: that when you have them and when you always keep to them they are harmful, but when you seem to have them they are useful, like seeming merciful, loyal, humane, upright and religious, and being so. But you must remain mentally prepared, so that when it is necessary not to have these qualities you are able, and know how to assume their opposites. It is essential to realise this: that a prince, and above all a new prince, cannot practise all those things which gain men a reputation for being good, as it is often necessary, in order to keep hold of the state, to act contrary to trust, contrary to charity, contrary to humanity, contrary to religion. It is for that reason that he needs a mind prepared to vary as the winds of fortune and free flow of events dictate, and, as stated above, he should not deviate from good if possible, but know how to act badly when necessary.

A prince should take great care, therefore, that nothing issues from his mouth which is not imbued with the five aforementioned qualities. To see him and hear him, he should seem all-merciful, all-trustworthy, all-integrity, all-humanity, all-religion. Nothing is more important to seem to have than this last quality. Generally speaking, men judge more by the eyes than by the hands, because everybody can see, but only a few can feel. Everyone sees what you seem, few feel what you are like. Those few do not dare stand against the opinion of the many who have the majesty of the state defending them. In the actions of all men, and most of all in princes, where there is no appeal to higher judgement, one looks to the result. A prince should seek to win and keep hold of a state. The means will always be judged honourable and praised by everybody, for the common people are always impressed by how things seem and by the way things turn out, and in the world there is nothing except common people. When the many are comfortably settled, the few will find no way in. A certain current prince, who had better remain anonymous, preaches nothing but peace and trust, and is an implacable enemy of both. If he had observed either of these qualities, he would have lost either his reputation or his state on several occasions.

CHAPTER 19

On the Avoidance of Contempt and Hatred
(De contemptu et odio fugiendo)

Since the qualities discussed above were only the most important ones, I would like briefly to consider the others under this general heading: that the prince, as hinted at above, should seek to avoid those things that render him odious and contemptible. Whenever he avoids them, he will have fulfilled his job and will find that his other evil actions pose no threat to him at all. As I have said, he will be hated above all if he is rapacious and seizes his subjects' property and women. He should refrain from doing this. The majority of men live happily so long as they are not deprived of either their property or their honour. The prince has only to contend with the ambition of a few which can be easily restrained in a variety of ways. He will be held in contempt if he is considered capricious, superficial, effeminate, cowardly and irresolute. A prince should avoid these things like the plague, and seek to show greatness, courage, gravity and strength in his actions, ensuring that his decisions in his subjects' private affairs are irrevocable and that he maintains such standing that nobody thinks to deceive or outwit him.

The prince who earns this reputation for himself is held in high esteem, and as long as he is understood to be a great man and revered by his subjects, it is difficult to conspire against and attack such a person when they are esteemed. For a prince should have two fears: an internal one, in regard to his subjects, and an external one, in regard to foreign powers. He defends himself against the latter with good arms and good allies, and when he has good arms he will always have good allies. Internal affairs will always remain stable whilst external matters are stable, unless they have already been disturbed by a conspiracy. And even when external circumstances change, if the prince has organised and conducted himself as I have said, and if he does not capitulate, he will always withstand any assault, as did Nabis the Spartan (as I mentioned). As regards his subjects, however, when external circumstances are stable he should be fearful lest they conspire against him. The prince can secure himself against this quite well, by avoiding being hated or despised and ensuring the people are content with him. It is vital to do this, as was made clear at length above. One of the most potent remedies a prince can have against conspiracies is not being hated by the population as a whole, because conspirators always hope to satisfy the people with the death of the prince. When they think they might offend the people, they are not courageous enough to begin such an enterprise, because the difficulties conspirators face are endless. Experience shows that there have been many conspiracies, but that precious few have turned out as planned. For a conspirator cannot act alone, nor can he associate himself with anybody except those he considers dissatisfied, and the instant he discloses his intentions to dissatisfied citizens, he grants them the means of satisfying themselves, for they can obviously then hope for all kinds of rewards. Consequently, any associate must either be an exceptional friend or a steadfast enemy of the prince if he is to keep faith with you, for, whilst informing guarantees profit, co-operation promises nothing but uncertainty and danger. To put it briefly, I maintain that from the conspirator's standpoint there is nothing but fear, envy and the dreadful possibility of punishment, while the prince has the majesty of being a prince, the laws and the support of his friends and the state on his side, all of which defend him. When the people's goodwill is joined to all these, it is impossible that anyone should be so bold as to conspire. While a conspirator is normally fearful before he carries out the evil deed, in this instance he must also be afraid after he has committed the crime (as he has the people as his enemy), and for this reason he cannot hope to find any refuge.

Endless examples could be cited on this subject, but I will satisfy myself with one in particular which occurred within our fathers' lifetime. Messer Annibale Bentivoglio, grandfather of the present Annibale and ruler of Bologna at that time, was murdered by the Canneschi who had conspired against him. Only messer Giovanni remained of his line, and he was still in swaddling clothes. The people rose up at once, and murdered all the Canneschi. This was due to the popular goodwill in which the Bentivoglio family was held in those days, which was so great that although, with Annibale's death, not one of that family was left in Bologna who could rule the city, the people of Bologna went to Florence to recall a person they heard had been born a Bentivogli. Until that point he had been raised as the son of an artisan. They conferred the government of the city upon him, and he ruled over Bologna until such time as messer Giovanni reached a suitable age for governing.[53]

[53] This episode is also related by Machiavelli in the *Florentine Histories*, VI,

I conclude, therefore, that a prince should pay scant attention to conspiracies so long as the people are well disposed towards him. But when they are his enemy and hold him in contempt, he must be fearful of everybody and everything. Well-organised states and wise princes have carefully sought not to deprive the nobles of hope and to satisfy the people and keep them happy, for this is one of the most important concerns that a prince has.

Amongst the well-organised and well-governed kingdoms of our own time is France. In it one finds countless good institutions, upon which the king's liberty and security depend. Foremost amongst these is the *parlement* with its authority. The man who established that kingdom recognised the ambition and insolence of the powerful, judging it necessary for them to have a bit placed in their mouths which could be used to control them. He also recognised that the people's hatred for the nobles was based on fear, and in seeking to reassure them he did not want this particular task to fall to the king, in order to save him from the nobles' displeasure should he favour the people, and the people's were he to favour the nobles. Consequently, he established a third party as judge, to beat the great and favour the small without the king being reproached personally. There could not be a better or more prudent institution, nor one more responsible for the security of the king and the kingdom. Another important point can be drawn from this: that princes should ensure that other people administer unpopular measures while the granting of favours remains in their own hands. Once again I conclude that a prince must value the nobles, whilst not making himself hated by the people.

To many people it might seem that an examination of the lives and deaths of certain Roman emperors furnish examples that contradict this opinion of mine, since some lived consistently distinguished lives, demonstrating great strength [*virtù*] of mind, and yet lost the Empire or were even murdered by their

Chaps. 9–10. The family members traced to Florence was Sante Bentivoglio (1426–63), a bastard son of Ercole Bentivoglio, who ruled Bologna until his death in 1463, when he was succeeded by the twenty-year-old Giovanni Bentivoglio.

own people who conspired against them. As I wish to reply to these objections, I will discuss the qualities of some of these emperors, showing how the reasons for their downfall are not out of keeping with the reasons adduced by me. I will choose for consideration events that are known to those who read about those times. I want all those emperors who succeeded to the Empire between Marcus the philosopher and Maximus to suffice, namely Marcus, Commodus his son, Pertinax, Julian, Severus, Antoninus, Caracalla his son, Macrinus, Heliogabalus, Alexander and Maximinus.[54]

The first thing to note is that whereas in other principalities there was only the ambition of the nobles and the insolence of the people to deal with, the Roman emperors had a third difficulty: they had to tolerate the cruelty and greed of the soldiers. This was so difficult that it caused the ruination of many, as it was hard to satisfy the soldiers and the people. For the people loved peace and consequently loved modest rulers, while the soldiers loved rulers who were military-minded and arrogant, cruel and greedy. They wanted their rulers to demonstrate these qualities on the people, so that they could double their salaries and give vent to their avarice and cruelty.

These considerations meant that those emperors who, either naturally or through their own efforts, lacked a strong reputation which enabled them to hold both parties in check, came to ruin. When the majority of them, and especially those who assumed power as political newcomers, realised the difficulty presented by these two different humours, they preferred to satisfy the soldiers, as they considered damaging the people of little importance. This policy was expedient, for such rulers cannot but be hated by somebody, and should therefore first ensure that they are not hated by everybody. When this proves impossible, they should seek as much as possible to avoid the hatred of the most powerful groups. Therefore, those emperors who needed more than normal levels of support as newcomers

[54] Machiavelli's source was Poliziano's translation into latin of Herodian's history, published in 1493, which spanned the years from AD 161 to 238.

more often allied themselves to the soldiers than to the people. Whether or not this was a profitable policy nonetheless depended upon their ability to maintain their standing with the soldiers.

The reasons mentioned above explain why Marcus, Pertinax and Alexander, men who lived modest lives and were humane and kindly, and were lovers of justice and enemies of cruelty, came to unfortunate ends, with the exception of Marcus. He lived and died most honourably only because he succeeded to the Empire by hereditary right and did not owe any debt of obligation for it either to the soldiers or the people. In addition, as he possessed many qualities [*virtù*] that earned him respect, he was able to keep both parties within limits throughout his life, and was never hated nor despised. Pertinax, on the other hand, came to grief at the very outset of his administration, for he was created emperor contrary to the wishes of the soldiers, who were used to living dissolute lives under Commodus and were unable to bear the honest life which Pertinax desired them to follow. For this reason he became hated, a hate which was augmented by the disrespect felt on account of his age.

It should be noted at this point that hatred is felt as a result of both good and evil deeds. However, as I said above, if a prince wants to keep hold of his state he is often forced not to be good, because when the group you judge necessary for your safe-keeping is corrupt, whether it be the people, soldiers or nobles, it is worthwhile adapting to their humour in order to satisfy them. In that instance good works are your enemy. But let us come to Alexander, who was of such goodness that amongst the other praiseworthy things that were attributed to him there is the following: that in the fourteen years he held the empire not one person was put to death without trial. Nonetheless, because he was despised, considered effeminate and seen as a man who allowed himself to be governed by his mother, the army conspired against him and murdered him.

Turning, in contrast, to the qualities of Commodus, Severus, Antonino Caracalla and Maximus: they are seen to have been very cruel and very greedy. For in order to satisfy the soldiers they inflicted every possible kind of injury on the people. All of them except Severus came to unfortunate ends. Severus, however, had such personal ability and strength [*virtù*] that in keeping the soldiers friendly towards him he was always able to reign happily, despite the fact that he oppressed the people. His personal abilities [*virtù*] made him so impressive in the eyes of both the soldiers and the people, that the latter remained dumbfounded and stupefied, and the former respectful and satisfied.[55]

Because his actions were notable and outstanding for a new prince, I want to demonstrate briefly just how well he knew how to use the character of the fox and the lion, whose natures, as I have said, it is necessary for a prince to imitate. As soon as Severus realised the Emperor Julian's indolence, he persuaded his army, which he was leading in Slavonia, that it was right for them to go to Rome and avenge the death of Pertinax who had been murdered by the Praetorian Guards. Under this pretence he led his army against Rome without disclosing his aspirations to the Empire, and was in Italy before anybody knew he had set out. When he arrived in Rome he was elected Emperor by a terrified Senate, and Julian was killed. After this beginning, Severus faced two remaining difficulties in securing his rule over the whole state. Firstly from Pescennius Niger in Asia, commander of the Asiatic armies, who had declared himself Emperor, and secondly from the West, where Albinus was also aspiring to the Empire. Since he judged it dangerous to declare himself an enemy of both men, he decided to attack Niger and trick Albinus. He wrote to the latter explaining how he had been elected Emperor by the Senate and that he, Severus, wished to share that dignity with Albinus. He sent him the title of Caesar and, with the agreement of the Senate, made him co-Emperor. Albinus accepted these things as true. But once Severus had beaten and killed Niger, and pacified the East he complained

[55] Septimus Severus (AD 146-211) became Emperor after the death of Pertinax and the brief reign of Didius Julianus. He defeated the two other claimants to the throne, killing Niger in 194, and defeating Clodius Albinus, the governor of Britain, in France in 197. He himself died in York in 211.

in the Senate on his return to Rome that Albinus had sought to murder him despite the benefits Severus had conferred on him. It was therefore necessary for him to go and punish his ingratitude. He then sought him out in France, and took from him both his state and his life.

Whoever examines this man's actions carefully, therefore, will find he was a ferocious lion and a most astute fox, observing also how he was feared and revered by everyone and not hated by the armies. It is not surprising that he was able to hold on to such great power as a newcomer, for his exceptional reputation always defended him from the hatred which his greed aroused in the people. His son Antoninus was also a man who had excellent qualities that rendered him remarkable in the public's view and pleasing to the soldiers. For he was a military man who tolerated all hardships and who despised delicacies and every other kind of effeminacy, something that endeared him to the soldiers. Nonetheless, his ferocity and cruelty were so great and unparalleled (since after countless individual murders he killed a large part of the Roman, and all of Alexandria's, population) that he became universally hated, and even began to be feared by those around him, with the result that he was murdered by a centurion in the midst of his army.

It is worth noting that princes cannot avoid deaths such as these, as they result from the determination of a single-minded will, and anyone who is not himself afraid of death can attack them. A prince need not be too fearful of such a death, however, as they are very rare. He must merely seek not to offend seriously any of those who serve him personally or who surround him in service of the state. This is what Antoninus did, killing a brother of the centurion in an offensive manner, and threatening him daily. However, he kept him in his bodyguard, a decision that was rash and self-destructive, and so it proved.

But let us turn to Commodus, who found it very easy to hold on to the Empire, for being the son of Marcus, he inherited it by right. All he had to do was follow in his father's footsteps and both the soldiers and the people would have been satisfied. But as he was cruel and brutal by nature, he sought to please the

armies and make them dissolute in order to practise his rapa-
ciousness on the people. In addition, he did not maintain his
dignity, often descending into the arenas to fight the gladiators
and do other base things not worthy of his imperial majesty,
and so became contemptible in the soldiers' eyes. As he was
hated by one side and despised by the other, he was conspired
against and killed.

We still have to recount the qualities of Maximinus. He was
a most warlike man who was elected Emperor by the armies
when they became tired of Alexander's effeminacies, which I
mentioned above. He remained Emperor for only a very short
time, as two things made him both hated and despised. Firstly,
he was of the most lowly birth, having previously been a
shepherd in Thrace (a fact that was remarked upon by everybody and meant that he was viewed by everyone with great
contempt), and secondly, since at the beginning of his rule he
delayed going to Rome to assume the imperial throne, having
gained a reputation for himself as being extremely cruel through
the actions of his prefects in Rome and elsewhere in the Empire,
as both he and the prefects had committed many cruelties.
Consequently, driven by the stigma of his lowly birth and by the
hatred of his fearful ferocity, the whole world rose up, with
Africa rebelling first and then the Senate backed by all the people
of Rome, and the whole of Italy conspired against him. His own
army also joined them, and while they were besieging Aquileia
and experiencing some difficulty in occupying the town they
killed him, as they were tired of his cruelty and were less fearful
of him once they saw how many enemies he had.

I do not want to discuss Heliogabalus, or Macrinus, or Julian,
who were destroyed ahmost immediately for being generally
despised, but come to the conclusion of this discourse. I maintain
that nowadays princes less often face the difficulty of having to
satisfy the soldiers under their command by extraordinary
means, because, despite the fact that they have to bear them in
mind to some extent, problems are nonetheless quickly resolved
because none of these princes have armies that have grown old
alongside the provincial governments and administrations, as

was the case with the armies of the Roman Empire. Besides, if it were necessary at that time to satisfy the soldiers more than the people, this was because the soldiers were stronger than the people. Nowadays it is more important for all princes, with the possible exception of the Turk and the Sultan, to satisfy the people more than the soldiers, as the people are more powerful.

I make an exception of the Turk because he always keeps a force of twelve thousand infantry and fifteen thousand cavalry around him, upon which depend both the security and the strength of his realm. It is therefore necessary for that ruler to set aside all other concerns if he wishes to maintain the friendship of the soldiers. Similarly, the Sultan's kingdom is wholly in the hands of the soldiers, and he must maintain their allegiance even at the people's cost. One also has to bear in mind that the Sultan's state is of a different form from all the other principalities, since it is similar to the Christian Papacy, which cannot be termed either an hereditary, or a new, principality. For the state is not inherited by and ruled by the sons of the former prince, but rather by someone elected to that position. Since this is an ancient provision, it cannot be called a new principality because it experiences none of the difficulties of the new ones, for although the prince is new, the institutions of that state are old and formulated to receive him as if he were an hereditary ruler.

But let us return to the matter in hand. I maintain that anyone who considers the above discourse will observe that either hate or contempt have been the cause of the aforementioned emperors' downfalls. He will also realise why it happened that when some emperors proceeded in one way and others differently in each of these groups, one person had a happy and the rest an unhappy ending. For it would have been useless and harmful for Pertinax and Alexander to imitate Marcus, as they were new princes and he was an hereditary prince. Similarly, it would have been harmful for Caracalla, Commodus and Maximus to imitate Severus, as they lacked the necessary personal ability [virtù] to follow in his footsteps. A new prince in a new principality, therefore, cannot imitate the actions of Marcus, nor is it necessary for him to follow those of Severus, but he must take those parts that are necessary for the foundation of his state from Severus, and those parts that are fitting and glorious for the conservation of an already established and secure state from Marcus.

CHAPTER 20

Whether Fortresses and Many Other Things Commonly Used by Princes are Useful or Useless
(*An arces et multa alia quae cotidie a principibus fiunt utilia an inutilia sint*)

Some princes, in order to hold on to their states securely, have disarmed their subjects, some have kept their subject towns divided, and some have fostered animosity against themselves. Others, on assuming the state, have sought to win over those they suspected; still others have built fortresses whilst others have ruined and destroyed them. And although one cannot pass a final judgement on any of these policies without examining the particulars of the states where such decisions were made, nonetheless I will discuss the matter in the general terms which seem fitting.

A new prince has never disarmed his subjects. On the contrary, finding them unarmed, he always armed them. For in arming them, they become his arms. Those whom you consider suspect become loyal, those who are loyal remain so, and your subjects become your supporters. And because it is impossible to arm all your subjects, when you favour those you arm, you can deal more securely with the others, for those you arm recognise the difference in the way you treat them, and this binds them to you more strongly. The others will excuse you, judging it necessary that those who face greater danger and are more at your disposal are treated more favourably. But when you disarm them, you start to offend them, for in doing so you demonstrate your distrust of them, either because of their cowardice or disloyalty. Both of these opinions will result in your being hated. Since you cannot remain unarmed, you are compelled to turn to mercenary troops, the characteristics of which are as noted above. No matter how good these troops are, they cannot be strong enough to defend you from powerful enemies and suspect subjects. Therefore, as I said, a new prince in a new principality has always organised military matters there, and examples of this are widespread in the histories.

But when a prince acquires a new state which he joins to his old one like a limb, it is then necessary for him to disarm that state, with the exception of those who were his supporters in acquiring it. In time, it is even necessary to mollify and emasculate these supporters when the opportunities arise, organising himself so that all the weapons in the state are in the hands of his own troops who were used to living by his side in the old state.

Our ancestors and those who were considered wise used to claim that it was necessary to hold Pistoia with factions and Pisa with fortresses, and consequently nurtured differences in several subject cities in order to keep hold of them more securely.[56] This policy must have been a good one during the times when Italy was, to a certain extent, balanced. But I do not think it can be considered a good maxim these days, as I do not believe that divisions ever do anybody any good. On the contrary, necessity dictates that when divided cities are approached by the enemy they are lost almost immediately, for the weaker faction will always adhere to the external forces, and the other faction will not be able to resist.

In my opinion, the Venetians, motivated by the reasons given above, nurtured the Guelf and Ghibelline factions in their subject cities, and although they never let it lead to bloodshed, they nevertheless fostered disagreements between them so that, bound up in their differences, those citizens would not unite

---

[56] Machiavelli's observations are based on the opinions recorded in the *Consulte e pratiche*, the minutes of the civic council meetings where the city's political élite, the ironically termed wise men, met regularly to discuss important civic business. Machiavelli mentions this maxim again in the *Discourses*, III, 27.

against Venice. That this did not subsequently turn out as planned is clear, for when they were routed at Vailà one of the factions there took courage, and seized the whole state from them. Such policies, therefore, suggest weakness in the prince, since a bold prince would never allow such divisions, for they are profitable only in times of peace when he can use them to govern his subjects more easily. When war comes, however, the weakness of such policies is exposed.

There is no doubting that princes become great when they overcome difficulties and obstacles that are placed in their way. Fortune, therefore, especially when she wants to make a new prince great (and new princes have more need to acquire reputation than hereditary ones), creates enemies and has them launch campaigns against such princes, so that they have to overcome them, thereby climbing higher up the ladders that their enemies have provided for them. Consequently, many conslder that a new prince, when he has the chance, should cunningly nurture some opposition, so that in overcoming it there is a subsequent increase in his standing.

Princes, and especially new ones, have found those men who were considered dangerous at the beginning of their rule more loyal and more useful than those who were initially trusted. Pandolfo Petrucci, the ruler of Siena, managed his state more with the help of those he had feared than with anyone else. But one cannot generalise about this matter, as it varies according to circumstance. But I will say this: those men who were enemies of the prince at the beginning of a principality, and who need somebody to rely on to maintain their own positions, are always easily won over by the prince. And the extent to which they are compelled to serve him loyally is in proportion to their need to erase the unfavourable impression the prince had formed of them by their actions. In this way the prince will always derive more profit from them than from those who in serving him too faithfully neglect his affairs.

Since the subject demands it, I do not want to fail to remind princes who have acquired states with the backing of insiders to ponder at length the reasons that have motivated those who lent their support. If it is not natural affection for the prince but solely disaffection with the previous state, the prince will maintain their friendship only with the greatest of effort and difficulty, as it is impossible for him to satisfy them. When he considers the reason for this thoroughly, examining ancient and recent examples, he will note that those men who were content with the previous state are much more easily won over as friends, even though they were formerly his enemies, than those who, not being content with it, became his allies and backed him in its occupation.

Princes, in order to hold their states more firmly, have traditionally built fortresses to act as a bridle and bit on those who might conspire against them and as a safe refuge from any sudden attack. I applaud this policy, because it has been used since ancient times. Nonetheless, in our own times messer Niccolo Vitelli was seen to destroy two fortresses in Città di Castello in order to keep hold of that state. When Guidobaldo, the Duke of Urbino, returned to his dominion, from which he had been expelled by Cesare Borgia, he razed to the ground all the fortresses of the province, thinking this would subsequently make it more difficult to lose that state. When the Bentivogli returned to Bologna they followed a similar course of action.[57] Fortresses, therefore, are useful or not, depending upon the situation at the time, and if they benefit you in one way they harm you in another. You can summarise the matter as follows: the prince who fears the people more than outsiders should build fortresses, but the prince who fears outsiders more than the people should ignore them. The castle which Francesco Sforza built at Milan has caused, and will cause, more trouble to the Sforza household than any other source of disorder in that state. The best kind of fortress, however, is not to be hated by the people. Because even though you have fortresses, if the people hate you they will not save you, for there is never a

---

[57] Pope Julius II destroyed the fortress of Porta Galliera after driving Giovanni Bentivoglio from Bologna in 1506. See note 36 and Chapter 11. See also *Duke Valentino's treacherous betrayal*, pp. 28–35 above, where Machiavelli also mentions Guidobaldo's destruction of the fortresses of Gubbio and Pergola.

shortage of outsiders ready to help the people when they take up arms. In our own times there are no examples of fortresses benefiting a ruler, except for the Countess of Forlì when her husband Count Girolamo was killed, because thanks to the castle she was able to resist the popular onslaught and wait for support from Milan and then re-establish her position.[58] At that time circumstances were such that outsiders were unable to aid the people. The fortresses were later of little use to her when Cesare Borgia attacked her and the people joined with him, as an outsider, against her. In the long run, therefore, she would have been safer not being hated by the people than having fortresses.

All things considered, therefore, I am prepared to praise princes who build fortresses and princes who do not, and blame anyone who places their trust in fortresses and considers being hated by the people of little importance.

CHAPTER 21
How a Prince Should Act in Order to Gain Reputation
(*Quod principem deceat ut egregius habeatur*)

Nothing makes a prince more highly esteemed than the assumption of great undertakings and striking examples of his own ability. In our own times we have Ferdinand of Aragon, the current King of Spain.[59] He can almost be called a new prince, as he has risen from being ruler of a small kingdom, through fame and glory, to be the foremost King in Christendom. If you consider his actions, you will see that they were all magnificent and some of them exceptional. At the beginning of his reign he attacked Granada, and the campaign provided the basis of his power. First, he launched it when he was undisturbed and had no fear of being obstructed, keeping the minds of the barons of

[58] Machiavelli recounts this whole story in the *Discourses*, III, 6. See Chapter 3.
[59] Ferdinand II of Aragon (1452–1516) 'the Catholic'. See note 3 above.

Castile occupied, so that in concentrating on the war they did not think of making political changes. In the meantime he was acquiring reputation and authority over them without their realising it. He was also able to establish armies with money from the Church and the people and, during the long war, he laid the foundations for his own military force which has subsequently brought him honour. In addition, to enable him to engage in more extensive campaigns, always under the cover of religion, he has employed a pious cruelty in tracking down and driving the Mariscos out of his kingdom, an example which could not have been more pitiful and extraordinary.[60] He attacked Africa under this same cloak of religion, launched the campaign in Italy, and recently assaulted France. He has always, therefore, performed and planned great schemes, which have always kept his subjects guessing and astonished, awaiting their outcome. And these feats of his have always followed hard on each other's heels, in such a way that people have never had the space to conspire quietly against him.

It is also quite profitable for a prince to give striking examples of his character in matters of internal government, like those recounted about messer Bernabò of Milan.[61] For, when someone does something extraordinary in civic life, be it good or bad, the prince can reward or punish them in such a way that it causes considerable discussion. Above all a prince should operate to secure a reputation for himself as a great man and a keen intellect in all he does.

A prince gains a greater reputation when he is either a true friend or a mortal enemy, namely when he backs one side against another without hesitation. This policy is always more useful than remaining neutral, since if two of his neighbours who are powerful rulers come to blows, they are either of a kind that will cause him to be fearful if they win or they are not. In

[60] The Mariscos were the Spanish Jews who were forced by the Inquisition to convert to Christianity. They were finally driven from Spain in 1502.

[61] Bernabò of Milan ruled the city between 1354–85, before he was poisoned by Gian Galeazzo. His bizarre and perverse punishments for miscreants were celebrated in Italian fourteenth-century collections of short stories or novellas.

either of these cases, it will be more profitable for him to declare his allegiances and enter into a genuine war. Because in the first instance, if he does not declare himself, he will always be at the mercy of the victor, much to the pleasure and satisfaction of the vanquished party. In addition, there will be nobody who will protect him or provide him with refuge, because the winner does not want suspect allies who will not help him in times of adversity. The loser will not receive him, as he was unwilling to take his chance with the eventual loser in armed combat.

Antiochus invaded Greece at the invitation of the Aetolians as they wanted him to drive the Romans out. He sent orators to the Achaeans, who were allies of the Romans, requesting they remain neutral. The Romans, on the other hand, were seeking to persuade them to take up arms on their behalf. The subject was presented for discussion in the Achaean council, where the orator sent by Antiochus persuaded them to remain neutral. The Roman legate replied to this decision as follows: 'Nothing is further from your interests than what they say about your non-intervention in the war, for you will be the victor's prize, without favour and without dignity.'[62]

It will always be the case that the person who is not your friend will seek your neutrality, while your friend will ask you to declare your armed support. Irresolute princes, in order to avoid current difficulties, normally assume the path of neutrality and are normally ruined as a result. But when you boldly declare your support for one side, if the person you back wins, although he is powerful and you are at his mercy, he is indebted to you and there is a bond of mutual support. In such instances, men are never so dishonest that they would crush you in a shocking display of ingratitude. Moreover, victories are never so clear-cut that the victors can ignore all considerations, especially as regards justice. But if the person you back loses, he will grant you refuge, and in helping you as much as he can, your shared fortunes may improve.

[62] Livy, *Ab urbe condita*, XXXV, 49. Another partially correct citation from Machiavelli's memory.

In the second case, when the combatants are such that you have no cause to fear the winner, it is even more prudent to commit yourself, for you help somebody ruin someone else. If your ally is wise he should be saving his opponent. For when he wins, he is at your mercy, and, with your backing, it is impossible for him to lose.

It should be noted at this point that a prince should never join forces with somebody more powerful than himself to attack another, unless he is compelled by necessity, as stated above, because when he wins he become a prisoner. Princes should avoid, as much as possible, being subject to another's will. The Venetians allied themselves with the French against the Duke of Milan. They could have avoided that alliance which led to their ruin. But when it is unavoidable (as it was for the Florentines when the Pope and Spain moved with their armies to attack Lombardy), then the prince should commit himself for the reasons mentioned above. No state should ever think it can always make secure decisions. On the contrary, it should consider all decisions it takes as risks, because it is in the nature of things that in seeking to avoid one difficulty you run into another. Prudence lies in understanding the nature of the difficulties, and taking the least problematic as best.

A prince should also demonstrate that he admires the virtues [virtù] of other people, encouraging men with ability [virtù], and honouring those who excel in a particular field. Similarly, he should encourage his citizens to believe that they can go about their business undisturbed, whether it be trading, agriculture or any other profession, so that one man is not afraid to increase his wealth for fear that it might be taken from him, and another is not afraid to start a business for fear of excessive taxes. For a prince should prepare rewards for those who want to do these things, or for anyone who thinks of any way to make his city or state greater. In addition, at the appropriate times of the year, he should entertain the people with celebrations and performances. And since all cities are divided into guilds or family groups he should bear these groups in mind, meeting with them periodically, showing himself to be humane and munificent whilst, nonetheless, always firmly retaining the majesty of his position, for this must be maintained at all times.

CHAPTER 22

On the Secretaries Who Accompany the Prince
(*De his quos a secretis principes habent*)

The choice of ministers is a task of no little importance for a prince. Whether they are good or not depends upon the prudence of the prince. The first impression one forms of a ruler's intelligence is based on an examination of the men he keeps around him. When they are capable and loyal, he can always be thought wise because he recognises them as capable and keeps them loyal. When they are otherwise it always gives a bad impression, since the first mistake he makes, he makes in this choice.

Nobody who knew messer Antonio da Venafro as the minister of Pandolfo Petrucci, prince of Siena, could help considering Pandolfo a most valiant person in having such a man as his minister.[63] For there are three types of intelligence: the first understands by itself, the second perceives what others understand, and the third does not understand by itself or with the help of others. The first is most excellent, the second good and the third useless. This necessarily meant that if Pandolfo was not in the first rank he was at least in the second. For whenever a prince has the ability to recognise the good or the bad that a person says or does (even if that person has no inventive spirit of his own), the prince can identify the bad and good works of the minister, praise the latter and punish the former. The minister cannot hope to deceive him, and consequently he continues to behave fittingly.

There is one infallible way, however, that you can recognise

[63] Antonio Giordani da Venafro was Professor of Law at the University of Siena before assuming political posts under Petrucci. He was Petrucci's representative at the fatal Diet of Magione. See Chapter 7.

the character of a minister. When you notice that the minister is more concerned with himself than with you, and that he seeks his own profit in all he does, such a person will never make a good minister, nor can you ever trust him. For the man who handles a state ruled by one person should never think of himself but always of the prince, and not bring anything to his prince's attention that does not concern him. For his part, the prince should consider the minister's needs in order to keep him loyal. He should honour him, make him rich, bind him with obligations, and include him in the distribution of honours and positions so that he sees that he cannot exist without the prince. In this way the many honours he has received do not make him desire more honours, the great riches do not make him desire more riches, and the many positions make him fearful of political changes. When ministers relate to their princes like this, and likewise princes to their ministers, there is mutual trust between them. When this does not happen, the result is always harmful for both parties.

CHAPTER 23
How Flatterers are Avoided
(Quomodo adulatores sint fugiendi)

I do not want to leave aside an important matter, a mistake that it is easy for a prince to make unless he is very prudent and has good judgement. This concerns flatterers, of which the courts are full, for men become so obsessed with their own affairs, deceiving themselves in the process, that it is difficult to defend themselves from this plague. In seeking to combat it, one runs the risk of becoming hated. There is no other defence against flattery than letting men know that they do not offend you by telling you the truth. But when everybody feels able to tell you the truth, you lose respect. A prince should therefore follow a third path, choosing wise men in his state who alone are given the freedom to speak to him truthfully, and only about those things he asks and nothing else. But he should consult them on all matters, and listen to their views, only then deciding on his own, as he sees fit. He should also comport himself with each of these advisers in such a way that each knows that the more freely he speaks the more readily he will be accepted. He should not listen to anyone except these few; he should follow up what has been decided and be resolute in his decisions. Anyone who acts differently either comes to grief amongst flatterers or changes his mind regularly because of the variety of opinions. This gives rise to his being held in little esteem.

Whilst on the subject, I want to cite a modern example. Father Luca, agent of Maximilian, the current Emperor, when speaking of His Majesty, reported how he never consulted with anybody, and nothing turned out as he planned. This was because he followed the opposite course to the one laid out above. For the Emperor is a secretive man who does not communicate his plans to anyone, nor does he take advice. But when put into action, these are gradually revealed and disclosed, and begin to be opposed by those who are around him, and because he is compliant he is dissuaded from pursuing them. Consequently, what is achieved one day is destroyed the next, nobody ever understands what he wants or plans to do, and they cannot rely on his decisions.

A prince, therefore, should always seek advice, but when he wants to and not when others see fit. Indeed, he should discourage people from advising him on anything, unless asked by him. However, he should be a keen and general enquirer, and then a patient listener to the truth concerning the matters he has asked about. Moreover, should he find anyone reluctant to tell him the truth for whatever reason, he should become angry. There is a widespread belief that some princes who have a reputation for being prudent in fact owe that reputation not to their own natural abilities but to the quality of the advice at their disposal. But this belief is quite unfounded. The following general rule is infallible: that a prince who himself is not wise cannot be well advised, unless by chance he should place himself in the hands of a most prudent man who manages all his affairs. In this case he might be well advised, but he would not last long, as the man who governs on his behalf would seize the state from him in no time. But when a prince who is not wise seeks advice from more than one person, he will never have a consensus of views, nor will he know how to establish one himself. Each of the advisers will consider their own concerns, and the prince will not know either how to punish such advisers or even to recognise them. They cannot be otherwise, for you will find that men always prove evil unless a particular need forces them to be good. So the conclusion must be that good advice, whoever gives it, had better arise from the prudence of the prince, rather than the prudence of the prince from the good advice.

CHAPTER 24
Why the Princes of Italy have Lost their States
(*Cur italiae principes regnum amiserunt*)

The above-mentioned things, if prudently executed, make a new prince seem long established, rendering him instantly more secure and more stable in the state, as if he had been there for a long time. For the actions of a new prince are under far more scrutiny than those of an hereditary one. And when those actions are recognised as virtuous, they captivate men far more, and bind them to him far tighter, than ancient blood. For men are much more taken by present things than past ones, and when they find the present to their liking they enjoy it and do not look for anything else. Indeed, they will defend him on all accounts, so long as he himself is not lacking in other respects. In this way he will enjoy twice the glory, having given life to a new principality and furnished it and strengthened it with new laws, strong arms and good examples. Similarly, a man who is born a prince and loses it through his lack of prudence incurs twice the shame.

If the rulers of our own time in Italy who have lost their states are considered – for example the King of Naples, the Duke of Milan and others, it is found they share a weakness, first of all in arms, for the reasons already discussed at length. Secondly, some of them had the people as enemies, or even if they had the people as friends, they did not know how to secure themselves against the nobles. For without these weaknesses states that are sufficiently strong to keep an army in the field are not lost. Philip of Macedon (not Alexander's father but the one defeated by Titus Quintius) possessed a small state in comparison with the power of the Romans and Greeks who attacked him. Nonetheless, because he was a military man who knew how to win over the people and secure himself against the nobles, he sustained the war against them for many years. And if he eventually lost his rule over a few cities, the kingdom nevertheless remained his own.

So these princes of ours who have held their principalities for many years only to then lose them, should not blame fortune but rather their own indolence, because having never thought that quiet times might change (a weakness shared by many men who fail to consider the possibility of a storm when times are calm) when the adverse weather then arrives, they think only of fleeing and not of defending themselves. They hope that the people, when they grow tired of the arrogance of the victors, will recall them. This policy is a good one when all else fails, but it is a very bad policy to abandon all others to follow this one. For one should never fall, believing someone will be found to gather one up. This either does not happen, or, if it does happen, it is not safe, as this kind of defence is cowardly and not dependent upon oneself. And the only defences that are good, that are certain and that are durable are those which depend solely on oneself and on one's own strength and ability [virtù].

CHAPTER 25
How Much Fortune can Influence Human Affairs,
and How She Should be Resisted
(Quantum fortuna in rebus humanis possit, et
quomodo illi sit occurrendum)

I am not unaware that many were, and still are of the opinion that human affairs are so governed by fortune and God that man is incapable of managing them with his prudence, indeed, that man has no remedy at all. They would therefore judge it worthless to sweat unduly over things, letting themselves be governed by chance. This belief has gained more credence in our own time due to the great changes that have been seen, and are still seen every day, things beyond human credibility. Sometimes when thinking about this, I am partially inclined to agree with their view. Nonetheless, in order that our free will should not be extinguished, I consider it possible that fortune is arbiter of half of our actions, but that even she leaves us to govern the other half. For she resembles one of those ruinous rivers which, when raging, floods the plains, destroys trees and buildings, and displaces earth from one place setting it down in another. Everyone flees before it, everybody submits to its impetus without being able to oppose it at any stage. And although this is the nature of rivers, it does not mean that men cannot make provisions during quiet times, by building both embankments and dykes so that when the waters rise they either run into a canal or their impetus is checked and less harmful. The same thing happens with fortune, for she shows her power where there is no force [*virtù*] marshalled to resist her, directing her impetus where she knows there are no embankments and dykes to contain her. And if you examine Italy, which is the heartland and originator of these changes, you will notice that it is a country without embankments and without a single dyke. But if she were protected by sufficient strength and wisdom [*virtù*], like Germany, Spain and France, either this flood would not have caused the changes that it has, or it would not have happened at all. I want this to be all that is said in general terms on the subject of resisting fortune.

But focusing my attention more specifically, I maintain that today one can observe a prince prospering one day and ruined the next without having seen him change his nature or character at all. I believe this arises primarily for the reasons laid out at length above, namely, that the prince who relies wholly on fortune is ruined as fortune changes. I also believe that the one who adapts the way he acts according to the quality of the times succeeds, in much the same way as the person whose way of proceeding is out of step with the times is unsuccessful. For men proceed differently in relation to the pursuit of their aims: namely glory and riches. Some proceed cautiously, others impetuously; some violently, others artfully; some with patience and others with its opposite. All of them can achieve their aims via these different methods. It can also happen that of two cautious men, one achieves his aim and the other does not, and similarly two men can be equally successful having followed different policies, one being cautious and the other impetuous. This is solely the result of the nature of the times which either does or does not conform with their way of proceeding. What I have said is based on this observation, that two people proceeding differently can achieve the same result, while of two people who proceed in the same manner one achieves his aim and the other does not. This also causes a variation in what is considered good, for if the times and circumstances evolve in such a way that a man's policy of governing with caution and patience is good, he continues to succeed. But if the times and circumstances change he will be ruined, because he fails to alter the way he proceeds. Nor will you find a man so prudent that he knows how to accommodate himself to this fact, partly because you cannot alter your natural inclinations, and also partly because when a person has prospered by following one path, you cannot persuade him to leave it. The cautious man, therefore, cannot act impetuously when the times demand it of him, and this leads to his ruin. Yet if he could change his nature according to the times and circumstances, his fortunes would not change.

Pope Julius II proceeded impetuously in all his affairs, and found that the times and circumstances so conformed to his way of proceeding that he always met with success. Consider the first campaign he launched, against Bologna, during the lifetime of Giovanni Bentivoglio. The Venetians did not approve of it, neither did the King of Spain. When he was still negotiating about the campaign with the French, he nonetheless personally launched that campaign through his own ferocity and energy. This move caught the Spanish and Venetians undecided and inactive, the former through fear, the latter because of their desire to recapture the Kingdom of Naples. On the other hand the Pope dragged the King of France in his wake, for the King seeing his move and, desiring to make an ally of him in his attempt to reduce the Venetians' power, judged that he could not deny Julius his troops without openly harming him. With his impetuous strategy, therefore, Julius accomplished what no other Pope, with the utmost human prudence, could ever have accomplished. For if Julius had waited until all his plans were completed and everything sorted out before leaving Rome, as any other Pope would have done, he would never have succeeded, because the King of France would have made a thousand excuses and the others would have planted a thousand fears in the King's mind. I will leave all Julius's other actions aside as they were all similar and equally successful for him, for it was the brevity of his life which prevented him from experiencing otherwise. If times had changed, however, and required him to proceed with caution, he would have been ruined. Nor would he ever have changed the way he acted as dictated by his character.

I conclude, therefore, that as fortune changes, and as men are set in their ways, they are happy so long as they get along together, and unhappy when they disagree. I consider the following very true: that it is better to be impetuous than cautious, because fortune is a woman, and it is necessary to beat her and maul her when you want to keep her under control. It is noticeable that she allows herself to be won over more by these types of men than by those who proceed dispassionately.

Therefore, as a woman, she is always a friend of young men, because they are less cautious, more brutal and command her with more boldness.

CHAPTER 26

An Exhortation to Seize Italy and Free her from the Barbarians
(*Exhortatio ad capessendam italiam in libertatemque a barbaris vindicandam*)

Having considered, therefore, all the matters discussed above, and personally thought about whether the current times in Italy are conducive to honouring a new prince, and whether the raw material exists which would give a prudent and able [*virtuoso*] prince the possibility of imposing some form which, in turn, might honour him and benefit the people of Italy at large, it seems to me that so many things are combining to the advantage of a new prince that it is difficult to imagine a more appropriate time to act. And if, as I said, a precondition of seeing the personal ability [*virtù*] of Moses was that the people of Israel were enslaved in Egypt, and that the greatness of Cyrus was recognised because the Persians were oppressed by the Medes, and the excellence of Theseus on account of the desperation of the Athenians, in the same way, in order to recognise the strength [*virtù*] of an Italian spirit, it is necessary that Italy is reduced to her current state: more servile than the Hebrews, more abject than the Persians, more scattered than the Athenians, headless, disordered, beaten, plundered, rent, overrun and having tolerated every kind of ruination.

And although a few have shown glimmerings of hope in the recent past, encouraging us to believe that they might have been ordained by God to redeem Italy, it has subsequently transpired that they have been spurned by fortune at the height of their endeavours. Consequently, Italy remains almost lifeless, waiting to see who may be the one to heal her wounds, put an end to the sacking of Lombardy, to the ransom of the Kingdom of

Naples and Tuscany, and treat her injuries which have already
been festering for a long time. Mark how she implores God to
send someone who can redeem her from these barbarous
cruelties and abuse. See how she is also well prepared and ready
to follow a standard, so long as there is someone who will bear
it. Nor can she hope in anyone at present more than your
illustrious house, which, with its fortune and ability [*virtù*], and
the support of God and the Church – which it currently heads –
can lead her to salvation.[64] This will not be very difficult if you
call to mind the actions and lives of those mentioned above.
And although they were exceptional and outstanding men, they
were nevertheless men, and each had less opportunity than exists
at present. Their undertaking was no more just than this one,
nor easier, nor was God more of an ally to them than he is to
you. There is great justice in this cause: 'for war is just for those
to whom it is necessary, and arms are sacred when there is no
hope except in arms'.[65] There is even greater readiness, and
where there is great readiness there is no great difficulty, so long
as your house aims to follow the methods used by those that I
have put before you. Moreover, extraordinary events are seen
here, events without precedent, carried out by God: the sea is
divided; a cloud has shown you the road; the rock has poured
forth water; manna has fallen from the skies; everything has
conspired to your greatness.[66] The rest must be done by you.
God does not want to do all things, so as not to deprive us of
free will and the part of that glory that belongs to us.

It is not surprising that none of the previously mentioned
Italians has been able to achieve what is hoped for from your

[64] Machiavelli is here making reference to the fact that Pope Leo X was
himself a Medici: Giovanni de' Medici, second son of Lorenzo *il Magnifico* de'
Medici.

[65] Livy, *Ab urbe condita*, IX, 1, 10. Machiavelli also cites this maxim in *The
Florentine Histories*, V, 8.

[66] The earlier reference back to Moses combines in this chapter with this
passage from Exodus 14:17 referring to the portents prior to the delivery of the
Israelites from Egypt. Machiavelli's paralleling of religious and political salvation
is reinforced by his use of the word '*redentore*', saviour, to describe his liberator
prince.

illustrious house, and that in the course of so many upheavals in Italy and so much warfare it always seems that Italy's military vigour [*virtù*] has been spent. This happened because its ancient military provisions were not good, and there was nobody who knew how to draw up new ones. And nothing brings a man who is recently come to power more honour than the new laws and the new institutions he devises. When these things are well founded and bear the mark of greatness he becomes venerated and admired. In Italy there is no lack of matter on which to impose any form. Here there is great strength [*virtù*] in the limbs, but it is lacking in the heads. See how this is reflected in duelling and skirmishes where the Italians are superior in strength, in agility and invention. But when it comes to armies, there is no comparison. This all results from the weakness of the heads, because those who do understand are not obeyed. Everyone thinks they understand although nobody to date has known how to rise up, either through their own abilities [*virtù*] or through fortune, and dominate the others. Consequently, during so much time, and so many wars fought over the past twenty years, whenever there has been an army composed wholly of Italians, it has always failed when tested, as witnessed by the battles of Taro, then Alessandria, Capua, Genoa, Vailà, Bologna and Mestre.[67]

If your illustrious house, therefore, wants to follow those outstanding men who liberated their lands, it is necessary, above all else, to furnish yourself with the true foundation of every undertaking: your own armies. For you cannot have more faithful, more genuine and better soldiers.[68] And although each of them is good in his own right, they will become better joined

[67] The River Taro was where Italian forces tried to prevent Chalres VIII from returning north at the Battle of Fornovo in 1495. The French forces of Louis XII plundered Alessandria and Capua in 1499 and 1501 respectively, took Genoa in April 1502 and defeated the Venetians at Vailà in 1509. In May 1511 they entered Bologna and returned the Bentivogli to power. In October 1513 Mestre was sacked by combined German, Papal and Spanish forces allied against Venice.

[68] Machiavelli's preoccupation with citizen militias was a lifetime concern. In 1506 he became Secretary to the Nine of the Militia established in Florence and wrote his *Discourse on Florentine Military Preparation*. Later in 1519 he wrote his *Art of War*. The passage that follows is reminiscent of the final section of his *Portrait of German Affairs* of 1508. See p. 20.

together when they see themselves led by their own prince, and honoured and maintained by him. It is necessary, therefore, to prepare these arms in order, with Italian strength [virtù], to defend ourselves against invaders. And although both the Swiss and Spanish infantry are considered formidable, they nonetheless both have weaknesses which would allow a third force not only to withstand them but also be confident of beating them. The Spanish cannot repel cavalry and the Swiss need to be fearful of the infantry when they encounter any as stubborn as themselves. Hence it is seen, and experience shows, that the Spanish cannot sustain French cavalry, and the Swiss are ruined by the Spanish infantry. And although there is no clear example of this latter case, nonetheless there was some indication of it during the battle of Ravenna, when the Spanish infantry confronted the German battalions, who use the same formations as the Swiss. In this instance the Spanish, using their physical agility and the help of their bucklers, passed under the German pikes and were safe in attacking them, while the latter had no means of defence. And if it had not been for the cavalry charging them, they would have killed an the Germans. So, having recognised the defects of both the Spanish and Swiss infantry, you would be able to form a new kind of infantry which could withstand the cavalry and not be afraid of the infantry. This would be achieved by using the right kind of weapons and altering the battle formations. These are the things which, newly instituted, grant a new prince esteem and greatness.

This opportunity must not be allowed to pass if Italy, after such a long time, is to see her saviour. Nor can I express with what love he would be received in all those provinces which have suffered from these foreign floods, with what thirst for revenge, with what resolute faith, with what devotion and tears. What doors would be closed to him? Which people would deny obedience to him? What jealousy would stand in his way? Which Italian would refuse him homage? Everyone thinks this barbarian tyranny stinks. May your illustrious house, therefore, assume this undertaking, with that courage and that hope which belong to all just causes, so that, under your standard, this

country may be ennobled and under her protection the saying
of Petrarch be fulfilled:

> prowess [*virtù*] against rage
> will take up arms, the combat being short:
> for ancient valour
> is still not dead within the Italian heart.[69]

[69] Petrarch, *Rime sparse*, 128, 93–9 [editor's translation]. 'Prowess' here
translates Petrarch's term *virtú*.

GLOSSARY OF WORDS AND TERMS

AMICO/AMICIZIA/OBLIGO, *Friend, friendship and obligation. The debate over the nature of true friendship was the result of anxiety concerning the moral rectitude of patron–client relationships and the dynamics of exchanging favours within renaissance society generally. Machiavelli's prince must seek to bind all his subjects to him, becoming the exclusive patron. By granting them favours, his subjects and advisers become his dependants. He himself, however, should not owe anybody, or be obliged to anybody, or be in anyone's debt. If he is, he should reverse the dependency to secure himself. In this context, Machiavelli also uses the term* amici *to refer to political and military allies.*

ASSICURARE/GOVERNARE/MANTENERE, *to secure, to govern, to maintain/hold on to. All these verbs relate to the prince's attempts to withstand fortune, prevent innovation within his own principality, and secure himself in power. They all involve controlling and restraining other forces, illustrating the underlying tension within the text.*

FORMA/MATERIA, *form and matter. The* materia *is the state, the raw material the prince acquires when he conquers a principality. It constitutes the social and political institutions, the religion, language, customs, and general culture of the principality, including its history. Hence a principality that has enjoyed freedom as a republic at some stage will prove more resistant to being formed by a new prince. An hereditary prince merely inherits a pre-formed principality. A new prince, however, will have to judge the extent of reform needed to secure himself within his new principality. Where possible and fitting, he should appropriate as much of the old form as possible.*

FORTUNA/VIRTÙ, Fortuna *is personified by Machiavelli as a woman, most extensively in Chapter 25. (See Introduction.) The manly quality of* virtù *is constantly at battle with her, seeking to control her. This contest is a consequence of Machiavelli's belief that we have 50 per cent control over our own destinies, the other half being at the mercy of Fortune. His use of the term* virtù *is more ambiguous, and is one of the defining characteristics of the piece. It is only rarely used as the opposite to vice (Chapters 15 and 8), more often referring to personal ability, strength, efficacy and power, both physical and mental. Although its actions may be immoral in the Christian sense, Machiavelli differentiates it from wickedness. Hence Agathocles in Chapter 8 cannot be included amongst great rulers because although he showed* virtù *in some of his actions, others were so wicked that they could not secure him fame and glory.* Virtù *would therefore, seem to have its own ethical status within Machiavelli's moral framework.*

INNOVARE/INNOVAZIONE, *to change or innovate: innovation, rebellion, uprising. These terms have a mostly negative evaluative sense in* The Prince. *They relate to political instability and the alteration of political forms. A prince seeking a new principality can profit from the instability caused by these changes, but once ruling must seek to prevent any kind of innovation within his own principality.*

NECESSITÀ, *necessity, is a key concept within the work, as it is the condition of necessity that compels a prince to act in a particular way. For Machiavelli necessary actions are those which if neglected would result in the ruination of the prince. There are a host of synonyms concerning the importance of the prince acting as necessity dictates: he is compelled, constrained, forced, obliged, bound, and he must, he has to and it is necessary for him to pursue particular policies.*

OCCASIONE, *opportunity or chance, is presented by fortune. Such opportunities are easily recognised by a* virtuoso *prince and are the cue for him to act, and one of the attributes which identify him as* virtuoso. *Having taken the opportunity, however, he must seek to minimise the opportunities for others to act against him.* Virtù, *therefore, also constitutes the ability to limit opportunities for others. See the final paragraph of* How to deal with the People of the Valdichiana who have Rebelled.

ORDINI, *institutions, provisions, formations, ranks, orders, customs, rules, laws, beliefs, procedures, ways, precepts. This is one of the most widely used words in* The Prince, *its meaning having to be decided by context. In the military sense it refers to formations, ranks or provisions. In the political sense it usually refers to institutions or governmental decrees, and in the social sense to customary activities. More generally it is used simply to refer to procedures.*

PRINCIPE/PRINCIPATO, *Machiavelli uses the term* Principe *to refer to any ruler who exercises political power, irrespective of lineage or social status. Hereditary princes were princes by right, but others could easily accede to the title, for example mercenary leaders and even private citizens. Machiavelli also sometimes uses the term* signore *in much the same way, to denote an absolute ruler within a small state of a monarchical type. Emperors, Popes and kings are all referred to by their titles. The* principato *is the dominion over which the ruler exercises authority, although Machiavelli also uses it in the sense of a position of pre-eminence, the headship of the principality.*

STATO, *state, is used in several ways by Machiavelli. It should not be read solely in the modern sense of a bureaucratic, independent and impersonal political entity, although Machiavelli does periodically use it in a way that suggests the political form is independent of the prince, that the people should be tied to the state. However, he also uses it to denote power and its acquisition, a position of authority, the study of politics, a geographical region, and a particular governmental form.*

Innocent Gentillet, *Discours contre Machiavel*, first published in France in 1576. The following passage is taken from Simon Patericke's translation of 1608 under the title, *A Discourse upon the meanes of well governing and maintaining in good peace a kingdome or other principalitie. Against Nicholas Machiavell the Florentine*, c.Aiiiv.

And whosoever also shall read the Maximes of Machiavell, which we shall handle hereafter, and discend from thence into the particularities of the French government, hee shall see that the precepts and maximes of Machiavelli, are for the most part, at this day practised and put in effect and execution, from point to point. . . . For are they not Machiavelists, Italians or Italianized, which doe handle and deale with the seales of the Kingdom of France?. . . . Yea, if a man will at this day obtaine or get any thing in the Court, for to have a good and quicke dispatch thereof, hee must learne to speake Messereske language, because these messers will most willingly heare them in their owne tongue; and they understand not the French, no, not the tearmes of iustice and Royall ordinances. Whereupon every man may coniecture and imagine how they can well observe, or cause to be observed the Lawes of France, the tearmes whereof they understand not. Moreover, plaine ynough it is, That within theses fifteene yeares, Machiavels bookes were as familiar and ordinarie in the hands of the Courtiers, as the Breviaries are in the hands of Curates of parishes.

A discourse made by William Thomas, esq. for the King's use: whether it be expedient to vary with time.
Thomas was made clerk of the Privy Council in 1550 after four

years in Italy and wrote the tract for the young King Edward
VI.

Truly as the musician useth sometime a flat, and sometime a sharp
note, sometime a short, and sometime a long, to make his song
perfect; so, saith Macchiaveghi [sic], ought man to frame his
proceedings unto his time. And albeit that man cannot so directly
concord them, as to make them always agree, like the musicians
divers notes, because some men are led of vehemence, and some
of respect and fear, in the one or other whereof al men most
commonly do err; yet he is to be esteemed the wisest and happiest
man, that in proceding maketh least discords with time. And as
the physician to the remedy of sickness ministreth both medecins
and diets, other than they should receive when they were whole;
so man in his affairs should procede according to his time, altering
as the occasion requireth; and not to persevere obstinately in one
opinion, how good or how profitable soever it had proved in other
time before.

James Bovey, *The Atheisticall Polititian or A Briefe Discourse
concerning Ni. Machiavell.* Written around 1642, Bovey cites
Machiavelli as a blameless observer of the evil of others, and
uses him as a measure of the corruption of Charles I's rule.

Nicholas Machiavell is cride downe for a villaine, neither do I
think he deserves a better title, yet when I consider he was not
only an Italian but a Courtier, I cannot choose but commiserate
his fortune, that he in perticular should beare the markes, which
belong to the wisest Statesmen in generall. . . . *Machiavell* saith,
what Prince had not rather be *Titus* than *Nero*, but if he will
needs be a Tyrant he shewes him the way that is least harmfull to
his temporall estate, as if he should say thou hast made thy selfe
already an enimie to God and thy people, and hast nothing to
hope for, beyond the honour of this world, therefore to keepe thee
from the fury of men, be sure thou art perfectly wicked. . . .
Neither are these rules he speakes of omitted in the best Kings, if
they be wise; for which of them doth not dispatch his ungrateful
actions by deputies; and those that are popular with his own
hands? doe any observe their promise so exactly as not to fayle

when they see the profit greater than can be expected at another
time ... is he to be blamed for setting downe the generall rules of
such Princes? Now if falsehood and deceit be not their true dialect,
let any judge that reads their stories? Nay cozenage is reduced
into so necessary an art amongst them; that he that knows not
how to deceive, knows not how to live. ... For a Commonwealth
is like a naturall body, and when it is all together shewes a comely
structure, but search into the entrals from whence the true
nourishment proceedes, and you shall finde nothing but blood,
filth and stench; the truth is, this man hath raked too farre in this,
which makes him smell as he doth in the nostrils of ignorant
people; whereas the better experienced know, it is the wholesome
savour of the Court, especially where the Prince is of the first
head.

Edward Dacre, *Nicholas Machiavel's Prince also the Life of
Castruccio Castracani of Lucca and the means Duke Valentine
us'd to put to death Vitellozzo Vitelli, Oliverotto of Fermo,
Paul, and the Duke of Gravina* (London, 1640), pp. A2r–A3r.
The following passage is taken from Dacre's dedicatory letter to
his patron, James Duke of Lennox and Earl of March.

Poysons are not all of that malignant and noxious quality, that, as
destructives of Nature, they are utterly to be abhord; but we find
many, nay most of them have their medicinall uses. This book
carryes its poyson and malice in it: yet mee thinks the judicious
peruser may honestly make use of it in the actions of his life, with
advantage. The Lamprey, they say, hath a venemous string runs
all along the back of it; take that out, and it is serve'd in for a
choyce dish to dainty palates. Epictetus the Philosopher sayes,
Every thing hath two handles, as the firebrand, it may bee taken
up at one end in the bear hand without hurt: the other being laid
hold on, will cleave to the very flesh, and the smart of it will pierce
even to the heart. Sin hath the condition of the firy end, the touch
of it is wounding with griefe unto the soul: nay it is worse; one
sinne goes not alone, but hath many consequences. Your Grace
may find the truth of this in your perusall of this Author: your
judgement shal easily direct you in finding out the good uses of
him: I have pointed at his chiefest errors with my best endeavours,

and have devoted them to your Graces service: which if you shall accept and protest, I shall remaine Your Graces humble and devoted servant Edward Dacres.

Anti Machiavel: or an Examination of Machiavel's Prince with notes Historical and Political, published by Mr de Voltaire, translated from the French (London, 1741), pp. 192–4. The author, 'who is said to be a Person of the highest rank', was in fact Frederick II, King of Prussia. The following passage is taken from his comments on Chapter 18 of *The Prince*, concerning the extent to which rulers should keep their word.

Machiavel the Preceptor of Tyrants, has the Boldness to affirm, that Princes may impose upon the World by Dissimulation. This is the first Position which I shall endeavour to refute. The extreme curiosity of the Publick is well known; it is a Being that sees everything, hears everything, and divulges whatever it has heard or seen. If its curiosity examines the Conduct of particular Men, 'tis only to fill up idle Hours; but if it considers the Character of Princes, 'tis with an Eye to its own Interest. And indeed Princes are more exposed than all other Men, to the Conjectures, Comments and Judgment of the World; they are a sort of Stars, at which a whole People of Astronomers are continually levelling their Telescopes and Cross-staves; Courtiers who are near them are daily taking their Observations; a single Gesture, a single Glance of the Eye, discovers them; and the People who observe them at a greater distance magnify them by Conjectures; in short as well may the Sun hide its spots, as great Princes their Vices and their genuine Character, from the Eyes of so many curious observers.

If the mask of Dissimulation should cover, for a time, the natural deformity of a Prince, yet he could never keep his mask always on; he would sometimes be obliged, was it only for a Breathing, to throw it off; and one View of his naked Features would be sufficient to content the Curious. It will therefore be in vain for Dissimulation to dwell in the Mouths of Princes; Craftiness in their Discourses and Actions will have no Effect: To judge of Men by their words and Professions, would be the way to be always mistaken; we therefore compare their Actions with one another, and then with their Words; and against this repeated Examination, Falsity and Deceit will find no Refuge: No Man can well act any Part but his own; he must really have the same Character which he would bear in the World: Without this, the Man who thinks to impose upon the Publick, imposes upon none but himself.

Jean-Jacques Rousseau, *The Social Contract*, trans. M. Cranston (Harmondsworth, 1982), p. 118. The extract is a note added by Rousseau to his 1782 edition.

Machiavelli was a gentleman and a good citizen; but being attached to the house of Medici, he was forced during the oppression of his country to disguise his love of liberty. The very choice of an execrable hero reveals his secret intention, and the antithesis between his principles in his book *The Prince* and those in his *Discourses on Livy* and *The History of Florence* proves that this profound political thinker has so far had only superficial or corrupted readers. The Pope's court strictly prohibited his book, which I can well believe, since that was the Court he depicts most plainly.

Jacob Burckhardt, *The Civilization of the Renaissance in Italy*, first published in 1860, trans. S. G. C. Middlemore (Harmondsworth, 1990), pp. 71–2.

But of all who thought it possible to construct a state, the greatest beyond all comparison was Machiavelli. He treats existing forces as living and active, takes a large and an accurate view of alternative possibilities, and seeks to mislead neither himself nor others. No man could be freer from vanity or ostentation; indeed, he does not write for the public, but either for princes and administrators or for personal friends. The danger for him does not lie in an affectation of genius or in a false order of ideas, but rather in a powerful imagination which he evidently controls with difficulty. The objectivity of his political judgement is sometimes appalling in its sincerity; but it is the sign of a time of no ordinary need and peril, when it was a hard matter to believe in right, or to credit others with just dealing. Virtuous indignation at his expense is thrown away upon us who have seen in what sense political morality is understood by the statesman of our own century. Machiavelli was at all events able to forget himself in his cause. In truth, although his writings, with the exception of very few words, are altogether destitute of enthusiasm, and although the Florentines themselves treated him at last as a criminal, he was a patriot in the fullest meaning of the word. But free as he was, like most of his contemporaries, in speech and morals, the welfare of the state was yet his first and last thought.

Benito Mussolini, *Prelude to Machiavelli*, in *Opera omnia di Benito Mussolini*, ed. Edoardo and Duilio Susmel (Florence 1951–62), vol. 20, pp. 251–4. The speech of 30 April 1924 was made prior to the eighty-eighth meeting of the Council of Ministers, and addresses Chapter 17 of *The Prince* which discusses men's cupidity [editor's translation].

Machiavelli does not delude himself and he does not delude the Prince. The antithesis between the Prince and the people, between the state and the individual is, in Machiavelli's perception, fated. What was called utilitarianism, pragmatism, and Machiavellian cynicism springs logically from that initial position. The word 'Prince' should be understood as 'State'. In Machiavelli's perception the Prince is the State. Whilst individuals tend to be deaf to society, driven by their egotism, the State represents organisation and limitation. The individual has a tendency to evade continually; to disobey the laws, not to pay taxes and not fight wars. Those that sacrifice their own egotism on the altar of the State – heroes and saints – are few in number. All the rest are in a state of potential revolt against the State. The revolutions of the seventeenth and eighteenth centuries attempted to resolve this friction that lies at the heart of all State-organised social structures by having power rise up as an emanation of the free will of the people. There is yet another fiction and illusion. Above all, the term 'the people' has never been defined. As a political body it is a mere abstract entity. Nobody knows where it exactly begins, nor where it ends. The adjective 'sovereign' when applied to the people is a tragic joke. The people at the very most delegate, but they certainly cannot exercise sovereignty.... There is, therefore, immanent, even in those regimes that were tailor-made in the *Encyclopedia* ... the friction between the organised force of the State and the tendency towards fragmentation on the part of individuals and groups. Regimes based solely on consensus have never existed, do not exist, and probably never will exist. Well before my already famous article 'Force and Consensus', Machiavelli wrote on page thirty-two of the Prince, 'This is why all armed prophets are victorious and the unarmed destroyed. Because people are by nature fickle, it is easy to persuade them of something, but difficult to secure them in that conviction. For this reason it is worthwhile being organised in such a way that, when they no longer believe, they can be made to believe by force. Moses, Cyrus, Theseus, and Romulus would not have been able to make the people observe their governmental forms for long if they had not been armed.'

Antonio Gramsci, *The Modern Prince*, in *Selections from the Prison Notebooks of Antonio Gramsci*, trans. and ed. Q. Hoare and G. Nowell Smith (London, 1971), pp. 125-7.

The basic thing about *The Prince* is that it is not a systematic treatment, but a 'live' work, in which political ideology and political science are fused in the dramatic form of a 'myth'. Before Machiavelli, political science had taken the form either of the Utopia or of the scholarly treatise. Machiavelli, combining the two, gave imaginative and artistic form to his conception by embodying the doctrinal, rational element in the person of the *condottiere*, who represents plastically and 'anthropomorphically' the symbol of the 'collective will'. In order to represent the process whereby a given collective will, directed towards a given political objective, is formed, Machiavelli did not have recourse to long-winded arguments, or pedantic classifications of principles and criteria for a method of action. Instead he represented this process in terms of the qualities, characteristics, duties and requirements of a concrete individual. Such a procedure stimulates the artistic imagination of those who have to be convinced, and gives political passions a more concrete form.

Machiavelli's *Prince* could be studied as an historical exemplification of the Sorelian myth – i.e. of a political ideology expressed neither in the form of a cold utopia nor as learned theorising, but rather by a creation of concrete phantasy which acts on a dispersed and shattered people to arouse and organise its collective will. The utopian character of *The Prince* lies in the fact that the Prince had no real historical existence; he did not present himself immediately and objectively to the Italian people, but was a pure theoretical abstraction – a symbol of the leader and ideal *condottiere*. However, in a dramatic movement of great effect, the elements of passion and of myth which occur throughout the book are drawn together and brought to life in the conclusion, in the invocation of a prince who 'really exists'. Throughout the book, Machiavelli discusses what the Prince must be like if he is to lead a people to found a new State; the argument is developed with rigorous logic, and with scientific detachment. In the conclusion, Machiavelli merges with the people, becomes the people; not, however, some 'generic' people, but the people whom he, Machiavelli, has convinced by the preceding argument – the people whose consciousness and whose expression he becomes and feels himself to be, with whom he feels identified. The entire 'logical' argument now appears as nothing other than auto-reflection on the part of the people – an inner reasoning worked out in the popular consciousness, whose conclusion is a cry of passionate urgency. The passion, from discussion of itself, becomes once again 'emotion', fever, fanatical desire for action. This is why the epilogue of *The Prince* is not something extrinsic, tacked on, rhetorical, but has to be understood as a necessary element of the work – indeed as the element which gives the entire work its true colour, and makes it a kind of 'political manifesto'.

Michael Oakeshott, *Rationalism in Politics and other essays* (London, 1962), pp. 29–30.

It has been said that the project of Machiavelli was to expound a *science* of politics, but this, I think, misses the significant point. A science ... is concrete knowledge and consequently neither its conclusions, nor the means by which they were reached, can ever, as a whole, be written down in a book. Neither an art nor a science can be imparted in a set of directions; to acquire a mastery in either is to acquire an appropriate connoisseurship. But what can be imparted in this way is a technique, and it is with the technique of politics that Machiavelli, as a writer, is concerned. He recognized that the technique of governing a republic was somewhat different from that appropriate to a principality, and he was concerned with both. But in writing about the government of principalities he wrote for the *new* prince of his day, and this for two reasons, one of principle and the other personal. The well-established hereditary ruler, educated in a tradition and heir to a long family experience, seemed to be well enough equipped for the position he occupied; his politics might be improved by a correspondence course in technique, but in general he knew how to behave. But with the new ruler, who brought to his task only the qualities which had enabled him to gain political power and who learnt nothing easily but the vices of his office, the *caprice de prince*, the position was different. Lacking education (except in the habits of ambition), and requiring some short-cut to the appearance of education, he required a book. But he required a book of a certain sort; he needed a crib: his inexperience prevented him from tackling the affairs of State unseen. Now, the character of a crib is that its author must have an educated man's knowledge of the language, that he must prostitute his genius (if he has any) as a translator, and that it is powerless to save the ignorant reader from all possibility of mistake. The project of Machiavelli was, then, to provide a crib to politics, a political training in default of a political education, a technique for the ruler who had no tradition. He supplied a demand of his time: and he was personally and temperamentally interested in supplying the demand because he felt the 'fascination of what is difficult'. The new ruler was more interesting because he was far more likely than the educated hereditary ruler to get himself into a tricky situation and to need the help of advice. But, like the great progenitors of Rationalism in general (Bacon and Descartes), Machiavelli was aware of the limitations of technical knowledge; it was not Machiavelli himself, but his followers, who believed in the sovereignty of technique, who believed that government was nothing more than 'public administration' and could be learned from a book. And to the new prince he offered not only his book, but also, what would make for the inevitable deficiencies of his book – himself: he never lost the sense that politics, after all, are diplomacy, not the application of a technique.

Maurice Merleau-Ponty, *Signs*, trans. R. C. McCleary (Evanston, 1964), pp. 217–18.

Machiavelli does not ask that one govern through vices – lies, terror, trickery: he tries to define a political *virtue*, which for the prince is to speak to these mute spectators gathered around him and caught up in the dizziness of communal life. This is real spiritual strength, since it is a question of steering a way between the will to please and defiance, between self-satisfied goodness and cruelty, and conceiving of an historical undertaking all may adhere to. This virtue is not exposed to the reversals known to moralizing politics, because from the start it establishes a relationship to others which is unknown to the latter. It is this virtue and not success which Machiavelli takes as a sign of political worth, since he holds up Cesare Borgia (who did not succeed but had *virtù*) as an example and ranks Francesco Sforza (who succeeded, but by good fortune) far behind him. As sometimes happens, tough politics loves men and freedom more truly than the professed humanist: it is Machiavelli who praises Brutus, and Dante who damns him. Through mastery of his relationships with others, the man in power clears away obstacles between man and man and puts a little daylight in our relationships – as if men could be close to one another only at a sort of distance.

The reason why Machiavelli is not understood is that he combines the most acute feeling for the contingency or irrationality in the world with a taste for the consciousness or freedom in man. Considering this history in which there are so many disorders, so many oppressions, so many unexpected things and turnings-back, he sees nothing which predestines it for a final harmony. He evokes the idea of a fundamental element of chance in history, an adversity which hides it from the grasp of the strongest and most intelligent of men. And if he finally exorcises this evil spirit, it is through no transcendent principle but simply through recourse to the givens of our condition.

Paul Ricoeur, *History and Truth*, trans. C. A. Kelbley (Evanston, 1965), pp. 257–8.

Much has been said of the evil of 'Machiavellism'. But should we take the *Prince* seriously, as it must be, then we shall discover that it is by no means easy to evade its problem: how to establish a new power, a new State. The *Prince* evinces the implacable logic of political action: the logic of means, the pure and simple techniques of acquiring and preserving power. The technique is wholly dominated by the essential political relationship between the friend and the enemy: the enemy may be exterior or interior, a nation, nobility, an army, or a counsellor; and every friend may turn into an enemy and vice versa. The technique plays upon a vast keyboard ranging from military power to the sentiments of fear and gratitude, of vengeance and loyalty. The prince, conscious of all the ramifications of power, the immensity, the variety, and the manifold measure of its keyboard, will be equipped with the abilities of the strategist and the psychologist, lion and fox. And so Machiavelli raised the true problem of political violence, not that of ineffectual violence, of arbitrary or frenetic violence, but that of calculated and limited violence designed to establish a stable state. Of course, one can say that by means of this calculation, inceptive violence places itself under the judgement of established legality; but this established legality, this 'republic', is marked from its inception by violence which was successful. All nations, all powers, and all regimes are born this way. Their violent birth then becomes reabsorbed in the new legitimacy which they foster and consolidate. But this new legitimacy always retains a note of contingency, something strictly historical which its violent birth never ceases to confer upon it. Machiavelli has therefore elucidated the relationship between politics and violence. Herein lies his probity and his veracity.

Isaiah Berlin, 'The Originality of Machiavelli', in *Studies on Machiavelli*, ed. M. P. Gilmore (Florence, 1972), pp. 147–206.

Few would deny that Machiavelli's writings, more particularly *The Prince*, have scandalised mankind more deeply and continuously than any other political treatise. The reason for this, let me

MACHIAVELLI AND HIS CRITICS

say again, is not the discovery that politics is the play of power –
that political relationships between and within independent com-
munities involve the use of force and fraud, and are unrelated to
the principles professed by the players. That knowledge is as old
as conscious thought about politics – certainly as old as Thucy-
dides and Plato. Nor is it merely caused by the examples that he
offers of success in acquiring or holding power – the descriptions
of the massacre at Sinigaglia or the behaviour of Agathocles or
Oliverotto da Fermo more or less horrifying than similar stories
in Tacitus or Guicciardini. The proposition that crime can pay is
nothing new in Western historiography. Nor is it his recommen-
dation of ruthless measures that so upset his readers: Aristotle had
long ago allowed that exceptional situations might arise, that
principles and rules could not be rigidly applied to all situations;
the advice to rulers in *The Politics* is tough-minded enough; Cicero
is aware that critical situations demand exceptional measures –
ratio publicae utilitatis, ratio status, were familiar in the thought
of the Middle Ages 'Necessity is not subject to law' is a Thomist
sentiment: Pierre d'Auvergne says much the same. Harrington said
this in the following century, and Hume applauded him. These
opinions were not thought original by these, or perhaps any,
thinkers. Machiavelli did not originate nor did he make much use
of the notion of *raison d'état*. He stressed will, boldness, address,
at the expense of the rules laid down by calm *ragione*, to which
his colleagues in the *Pratiche Fiorentine*, and perhaps the Oricellari
Gardens, may have appealed. So did Leon Battista Alberti when
he declared that *fortuna* crushes only the weak and propertyless;
so did contemporary poets; so, too, in his own fashion, did Pico
della Mirandola in his great apostrophe to the powers of man,
who, unlike the angels, can transform himself into any shape, –
the ardent image which lies at the heart of European humanism in
the North as well as the Mediterranean.

Far more original, as has often been noted, is Machiavelli's
divorce of political behaviour as a field of study from the
theological world picture in terms of which this topic was discussed before him (even by Marsilio) and after him. Yet it is not
his secularism, however audacious in his own day, that could have
disturbed the contemporaries of Voltaire or Bentham or their
successors. What shocked them is something different.

Machiavelli's cardinal achievement is, let me repeat, his

uncovering of an insoluble dilemma, the planting of a permanent question mark in the path of posterity. It stems from his *de facto* recognition that ends equally ultimate, equally sacred, may contradict each other, that entire systems of value may come into collision without possibility of rational arbitration, and that not merely in exceptional circumstances, as a result of abnormality or accident or error – the clash of Antigone and Creon or in the story of Tristan – but (this was surely new) as part of the normal human situation. For those who look on such collisions as rare, exceptional and disastrous, the choice to be made is necessarily an agonising experience for which, as a rational being, one cannot prepare (since no rules apply). But for Machiavelli, at least of *The Prince*, *The Discourses*, *Mandragola*, there is no agony. One chooses as one chooses because one knows what one wants, and is ready to pay the price.

Antony Jay, *Management and Machiavelli: Power and Authority in Business Life* (London, revised edn, 1987), p. 18. The passage in quotation marks is the author's adaptation of a section of Chapter 3 of *The Prince* concerning the sending of colonies to conquered territories.

In other words, 'Put small management teams of your own into one or two key factories, because otherwise you'll use up half your staff in giving orders and issuing requests, and then checking that they've been properly fulfilled. By comparison a management team does not cost much, and the only people who will be upset are the former managers whose jobs they have taken over. And since they are no longer in the firm they cannot cause any trouble, while the rest of the staff will not protest as long as they still have their old jobs, particularly while they have the example of the sacked managers to keep them on their toes. The guiding principle is that senior men in taken-over firms should either be warmly welcomed and encouraged, or sacked; because if they are sacked they are powerless, whereas if they are simply downgraded they will remain united and resentful and determined to get their own back.' This, though Machiavelli does not mention it in this context, is the principle on which the Romans founded their Empire (which was one of the most spectacular examples of successful large-scale management); generosity (full Roman citizenship) or brutality (executions and enslavement, full military garrisons) but not the sort of half-hearted severity that left the defeated enemy resentful and still in being. Since reading that passage I have tried out Machiavelli's principle on several managers who have had to cope with take-overs; they are with him to a man.

SUGGESTIONS FOR FURTHER READING

Bibliography

S. R. Fiore, *Niccolò Machiavelli: An Annotated Bibliography of Modern Criticism and Scholarship* (New York, 1990).

Life

O. Tommasini, *La vita e gli scritti di Niccolò Machiavelli*, 2 vols (Rome, Turin and Florence, 1883–1911).

P. Villari, *The Life and Times of Niccolò Machiavelli*, trans. L. Villari, 2 vols, 4th edn (New York, 1969).

R. Ridolfi, *Vita di Niccolò Machiavelli*, 7th edn (Florence, 1978).

S. de Grazia, *Machiavelli in Hell* (Princeton, 1989).

Works

Niccolò Machiavelli, *Tutte le opere*, ed. M. Martelli (Florence 1971).

Niccolò Machiavelli, *Legazioni, commissarie, scritti di governo*, ed. F. Chiappelli and J. J. Marchand, 4 vols (Rome and Bari, 1971–85)

Niccolò Machiavelli, *Lettere (Opere di Niccolò Machiavelli*, vol. 3), ed. F. Gaeta (Turin, 1984).

Niccolò Machiavelli, *The Chief Works and Others*, trans. A. Gilbert, 3 vols (Durham, N.C., 1965).

Political and social context

J. R. Hale, *Machiavelli and Renaissance Italy* (English Universities Press, 1961).

N. Rubinstein, *The Government of Florence under the Medici (1434–1494)* (Oxford, 1966): 5–28.

N. Rubinstein, 'Machiavelli and the World of Florentine Politics', in *Studies on Machiavelli*, ed. M. P. Gilmore (Florence, 1972).

D. Kent, 'The Florentine *Reggimento* in the Fifteenth Century', *Renaissance Quarterly*, 28 (1975): 575–638.

H. C. Butters, *Governors and Government in Early Sixteenth-Century Florence, 1502–1519* (Oxford, 1985).

J. N. Stephens, *The Fall of the Florentine Republic, 1512–1530* (Oxford, 1983).

G. Brucker, *Renaissance Florence* (New York, 1969).

R. Trexler, *Public Life in Renaissance Florence* (New York, 1980).

Intellectual context

The Cambridge History of Renaissance Philosophy, ed. C. B. Schmitt and Q. Skinner (Cambridge, 1988).

The Cambridge History of Early Modern Political Thought, ed. J. H. Burns (Cambridge, 1991).

B. P. Copenhaver and C. B. Schmitt, *Renaissance Philosophy* (*A History of Western Philosophy*, 3) (Oxford, 1992).

Renaissance Humanism: Foundations, Forms and Legacy, ed. A. Rabil Jnr, 3 vols (Philadelphia, 1988).

H. Baron, *The Crisis of the Early Italian Renaissance*, revised edn (Princeton, 1966).

P. O. Kristeller, *Renaissance Thought*, 2 vols (New York, 1961–5).

F. Gilbert, 'Florentine Political Assumptions in the Age of Savonarola and Soderini', *Journal of the Warburg and Courtauld Institutes*, 20 (1957): 187–214.

The Prince and early writings

A. Gilbert, *Machiavelli's 'Prince' and its forerunners* (Durham, N.C., 1938).

H. Baron, 'Machiavelli: The Republican Citizen and the Author of *The Prince*', *English Historical Review*, 76 (1961): 217–53.

F. Gilbert, *Machiavelli and Guicciardini* (Princeton, 1979).

M. P. Gilmore (ed.), *Studies on Machiavelli* (Florence, 1972).

Q. Skinner, *Machiavelli* (Oxford, 1981).

M. McCanles, *The Discourse of 'Il Principe'* (Malibu, 1983).

J. M. Najemy, *Discourses of Power and Desire in the Machiavelli-Vettori Letters of 1513–1515* (Princeton, 1993).

J. G. A. Pocock, *The Machiavellian Moment: Florentine Political Thought and the Atlantic Republican Tradition* (Princeton, 1975), pp. 156–82.

H. F. Pitkin, *Fortune is a Woman: Gender and Politics in the Thought of Niccolò Machiavelli* (Berkeley, 1984).

ACKNOWLEDGEMENTS

I would like to thank my colleagues at Bristol University, Judith Bryce, Derek Duncan and Antony Antonovics for their kind advice and comments, and Audrey Milner for helping with the proofs.

The editor and publishers wish to thank the following for permission to use copyright material:

Lawrence & Wishart Ltd for material from Antonio Gramsci, 'The Modern Prince' in *Selections from the Prison Notebooks of Antonio Gramsci*, trans. and ed. by Q. Hoare and G. Nowell Smith, 1971, pp. 125–7;

Routledge for material from Michael Oakeshott, *Rationalism in Politics and other essays*, Methuen & Co, 1962, pp. 29–30.

Every effort has been made to trace all the copyright holders but if any have been inadvertently overlooked the publishers will be pleased to make the necessary arrangement at the first opportunity.

PHILOSOPHY AND RELIGIOUS WRITING IN EVERYMAN

A SELECTION

Ethics
SPINOZA
Spinoza's famous discourse on the power of understanding £4.99

Critique of Pure Reason
IMMANUEL KANT
The capacity of the human intellect examined £6.99

A Discourse on Method, Meditations, and Principles
RENÉ DESCARTES
Takes the theory of mind over matter into a new dimension £4.99

Philosophical Works including the Works on Vision
GEORGE BERKELEY
An eloquent defence of the power of the spirit in the physical world £4.99

Utilitarianism, On Liberty, Considerations on Representative Government
J. S. MILL
Three radical works which transformed political science £5.99

Utopia
THOMAS MORE
A critique of contemporary ills allied with a visionary ideal for society £3.99

An Essay Concerning Human Understanding
JOHN LOCKE
A central work in the development of modern philosophy £5.99

Hindu Scriptures
The most important ancient Hindu writings in one volume £6.99

Apologia Pro Vita Sua
JOHN HENRY NEWMAN
A moving and inspiring account of a Christian's spiritual journey £5.99

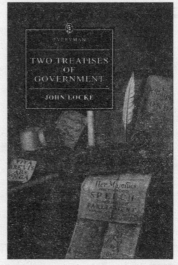

£3.99